# THE GREAT EJECTION

# THE GREAT EJECTION

## GARY BRADY

EP BOOKS
Faverdale North
Darlington, DL3 0PH, England

e-mail: sales@epbooks.org
**www.epbooks.org**

First published 2012
*Second impression October 2012*

**British Library Cataloguing in Publication Data available**

ISBN 13: 978-0-85234-802-4

Printed and bound in Great Britain by the MPG Books Group

# CONTENTS

To Chris Buckingham

# PREFACE

**W**hy remember the Great Ejection of 1662? Fifty years ago, in 1962, Dr D. Martyn Lloyd-Jones raised that question when giving the annual lecture of the Evangelical Library in London. His main argument for doing so was that practically all that is good in evangelicalism finds its roots in the Puritanism that was so fiercely persecuted in the Great Ejection and the oppression that followed.

He also added that 'the very greatness of the men themselves as men of God demands our attention'. While wanting to be impartial, he wanted to stimulate and invigorate faith by looking at what happened to them. This book is written in the same spirit.

Lloyd-Jones's views echo those of C. H. Spurgeon just over a hundred years before. Preaching on Samson in 1858, he said:

> Those great preachers whose names we remember, were men who

counted nothing their own. They were driven out from their bene-
fices, because they could not conform to the Established Church,
and they gave up all they had willingly to the Lord. They were
hunted from place to place … they wandered here and there to
preach the gospel to a few poor sheep, being fully given up to their
Lord. Those were foul times; but they promised they would walk
the road fair or foul, and they did walk it knee-deep in mud; and
they would have walked it if it had been knee-deep in blood too.

In 1912, a little book appeared called *The Great Ejectment of 1662*.
Benjamin Millard's purpose in writing it was to tell,

> … as simply and directly as possible, the story of the Ejectment
> from the Church of England of the Nonconforming Ministers
> of 1662; to give some idea of the sufferings they endured as a
> result of their loyalty to conscience; and to indicate the principles
> involved in their conflict with the Government and the Bishops.

Again, in 2012, our aim is similar. Christian churches existed
outside the national church in England before 1662 but it was
only when large numbers of Puritans from within the established
church 'threw in their lot with the despised sectaries' that Dissent,
or Nonconformity, became a force to be reckoned with.

In the nineteenth century Bishop J. C. Ryle wrote of the Great
Ejection, from an Anglican point of view, as miserable, disgraceful
and suicidal. 'A more impolitic and disgraceful deed never disfigured
the annals of a Protestant Church,' he wrote. It did 'an injury to
the cause of true religion in England, which will probably never
be repaired'. He felt, therefore, that we should all 'know something
about the subject, because it serves to throw immense light on the
history of our unhappy religious divisions in this country'.

As a Nonconformist, I have long been vaguely aware of the events
of 1662. My desire to discover more has been frustrated by a lack
of readily available material on the subject. Unsurprisingly, given
the difficulties, such ignorance appears to be widespread within
Nonconformity and beyond.

In this year, which marks the 350<sup>th</sup> anniversary of the event, it seemed appropriate, therefore, to attempt to do something to remedy this state of affairs. Hence, this short book on what Iain Murray has called a 'spiritual watershed which divides two eras of our religious history'. I trust it will inform and stimulate not only Nonconformists but all sorts of others too. An Internet blog has also been created, which can be found at www.greatejection.blogspot.com.

We will begin with a chapter that seeks to whet the appetite for looking at those times with some stories from the period. We will then briefly outline England's religious history across the long period from the Reformation to the dawn of the Great Ejection, with our focus firmly on the Puritan movement.

Chapter 3 deals with the period from Charles's accession to the dawn of the Great Ejection, with the following chapter looking at the Great Ejection itself. Chapter 5 looks at the subsequent acts that ratcheted up the sufferings of Nonconformists following the ejection and how they suffered. In another chapter, we will also say something about the 1689 Act of Toleration and some of the previous efforts made to bring about such a toleration.

In Chapters 7 we will consider the farewell sermons that the ejection prompted from many of the Dissenters and then, in Chapters 8 and 9, some of the individuals directly affected by the ejections. Throughout the book I have tried, where possible, to give the date of the birth and death of most individuals as a help to keeping track of things. A timeline has also been added with a similar purpose in mind.

Finally, in a closing chapter we will attempt to briefly draw some practical conclusions from the history of the period that will have relevance to us today, 350 years later and beyond.

Gary Brady
April 2012

# ACKNOWLEDGEMENTS

I grew up on a housing estate in South Wales. When I was five years old there was hardly a building there very much older than I was. A hundred yards round the corner from my door, however, was a magnificent Nonconformist chapel with a Nonconformist graveyard that was a lot older indeed. The chapel had been built in 1836, the work having begun in 1815. To my young eyes the chapel looked something like an alien spaceship landed in the middle of our modern world. That is where I first heard about Jesus Christ and faith in him and became a Christian, a Baptist and a Nonconformist.

Since those days I must have worshipped in a hundred or more such chapels and for the last twenty-eight years or so I have preached regularly in a Nonconformist chapel in my role as pastor of a Nonconformist church (rather less attractive and distinct, this one went up in 1870). Further, a large chunk of my reading and study has been in the Nonconformist milieu. I have been immersed in Nonconformity all my life and my debt to the movement, under God, is incalculable.

For many years I have studied Puritan and Nonconformist history and have benefited not only from more formal studies through the LTS and the John Owen Centre but also from the annual Westminster Conference held in London every December.

In spending time more specifically on studying the origins of the movement and preparing this book for the press I have had a great deal of help, both direct and indirect. Here I would particularly like to acknowledge help with reading matter from the good people at Wikipedia, Google and Amazon and that fine institution the Evangelical Library. Also, individuals who have provided encouragement, comment and the loan of books, especially Geoff Thomas, Norman Hopkins and Robert Strivens.

EP Books have again been a great help, especially the irrepressible Erroll Hulse.

As ever, I would also like to acknowledge the support of the church here in Childs Hill and of my family situated both near and far. The book is dedicated to my friend of forty years Chris Buckingham. Don't you remember the days of the old graveyard?

# 1 | OF PRISONS, ALEHOUSES AND SHEEP — STORIES FROM THE PERIOD

**O**ur focus in this book will chiefly be on those who were ejected from the Church of England, mainly in 1662, rather than on those who chose to be Separatists, although both sorts of believer suffered during the period. It is with a quotation from a Separatist, however, that we want to begin, one that was written in a prison.

John Bunyan (1628-88), the famous author of *The Pilgrim's Progress*, wrote a book on prayer in that fateful year of 1662. In it, he urges us to 'look into the gaols in England, and into the alehouses of the same' and suggests that if we do so, we will find 'those that plead for the Spirit of prayer in the gaol, and them that look after the form of men's inventions only in the alehouse'.

No doubt Bunyan employs justifiable hyperbole here but there was more than a grain of truth in what he wrote as far as the years 1660 to 1689 are concerned. We all like stories and before we look at some of the detail from the period we can gain something of the flavour of the times by considering a few examples.

## Prisons

Bunyan was himself in the Bedford county jail for Nonconformity when he was writing. He had been imprisoned under the terms of the 1593 Religion Act of Elizabeth I's reign. Arrested in November 1660, he would remain in prison until 1672, though with a certain amount of freedom to come and go.

He was not the only one. Some 120 miles south-west of Bedford is the town of Ilchester, Somerset. In May 1663, we find there another man of God incarcerated alongside several others of like-mind, men with a preference for 'the Spirit of prayer' over 'the inventions of men'.

Joseph Alleine (1634-68), author of the posthumous bestseller *Alarm to the Unconverted* (also known as *A Sure Guide to Heaven*), is less well known than Bunyan but he was also the Lord's prisoner. His older brother Edward, a minister, died in 1645 aged only twenty-six, prompting Joseph also to become a minister in Taunton, where he worked alongside Devonian George Newton (1602-81). Newton, 'a plain, profitable and successful preacher, eminent for meekness and prudence', was also ejected in 1662.

In 1655 Alleine had married his cousin, Theodosia Alleine (*fl.* 1654-77). She was the daughter of Richard Alleine (1610-81), the ejected rector of Batcombe and author of the widely read *A Vindication of Godliness*. His younger brother William Alleine (1613/14-77) was ejected from Blandford, Somerset, in 1661. Theodosia subsequently wrote of her husband that

He would be much troubled if he heard smiths or shoemakers, or such tradesmen, at work at their trades, before he was in his duties with God: saying to me often, 'O how this noise shames me! Doth not my Master deserve more than theirs?'

She also described how he came to be in prison. She tells how the two of them were at home in Taunton one Saturday evening when at about six o'clock

... my husband was seized on by an officer of our town, who would rather have been otherwise employed, as he hath often said, but that he was forced to a speedy execution of the warrant by a justice's clerk, who was sent on purpose with it to see it executed, because he feared that none of the town would have done it.

The warrant, signed by three Justices, required Alleine to appear at one of their houses, about two miles out of town. He asked if he could eat with his family first — he and his wife had a young daughter called Isabella. This was initially denied but a prominent man in the town agreed to guarantee his speedy appearance after that. Theodosia continues:

His supper being prepared, he sat down, eating very heartily, and was very cheerful, but full of holy and gracious expressions, suitable to his and our present state.

After supper, having prayed with the family, he went with the officer and two or three friends to the Justice's house, where he was accused of breaking the law by preaching, which he denied. He was then accused of 'being at a riotous assembly' though he had been involved in nothing but preaching and prayer.

Then he was much abused with many scorns and scoffs from the justices and their associates, and even the ladies as well as the gentlemen often called him rogue, and told him that he deserved to be hanged, and if he were not, they would be hanged for him, with many such like scurrilous passages, which my husband receiving with patience, and his serene countenance showing that he did slight the threatenings, made them the more enraged. They then urged him much to accuse himself, but in vain.

Despite a lack of evidence — and after keeping him until twelve o'clock with their abuse and mocking — they made out a *mittimus*, or arrest warrant, committing him to jail the following Monday. It was about two in the morning by the time he was home so he did not undress but lay on his bed to sleep for a few hours before rising to pray at about eight o'clock, by which time several friends had arrived. He was not allowed to preach but was free to speak with the various groups that flocked in from the town and nearby villages and to pray with them. Theodosia continues:

> He was exceeding cheerful in his spirit, full of admiration of the mercies of God, and encouraging all that came to be bold, and venture all for the Gospel and their souls, notwithstanding what was come upon him for their sakes. For, as he told them, he was not at all moved at it, nor did in the least repent of anything he had done, but accounted himself happy under that promise Christ makes to his, in the 5th of Matthew, that he should be doubly and trebly blessed now he was to suffer for his sake; and was very earnest with his brethren in the ministry that came to see him, that they would not in the least desist when he was gone, that there might not be one sermon the less in Taunton; and with the people, to attend the ministry with greater ardency, diligence, and courage than before; assuring them how sweet and comfortable it was to him to consider what he had done for God in the months past; and that he was going to prison full of joy, being confident that all these things would turn to the furtherance of the Gospel, and the glory of God.

Not wanting to leave his people without some final words, Alleine met with them in the small hours of the following morning. Several hundred gathered and he preached and prayed with them for about three hours.

He prayed for his enemies 'that God would not lay this sin of theirs to their charge'. The greatest harm that he did wish to any of them was 'that they might thoroughly be converted and sanctified, and that their souls might be saved in the day of the Lord Jesus'.

And so, with his yearnings towards his people, and theirs towards him, they took their farewell of each other — a more affectionate parting could not well be.

At about nine, again with friends accompanying him, he set out for Ilchester. The streets were lined with people on either side. Many followed him out of the town on foot for several miles, earnestly lamenting their loss. Alleine was very moved by all this but did his best to look cheerful and say something to encourage them.

> He carried his mittimus himself, and had no officer with him. When he came to the gate of the prison, finding the gaoler absent, he took that opportunity of preaching once more before he entered, which was afterwards considered a great aggravation to his former crimes. When the gaoler came, he delivered his mittimus, and was clapped up in the Bridewell chamber, which is over the common gaol.

On arriving, Alleine found there John Norman (1622-69) of Bridgwater. Norman, Alleine's Devon-born friend, had been imprisoned a few days before. He had probably been married to Alleine's sister Elizabeth, who died in about 1650.

Mrs Alleine bravely chose to share imprisonment with her husband, who was to spend the next four months in this hole. At that time the jail held fifty Quakers, seventeen Baptists and about twelve other ministers who, like Alleine, had been arrested for preaching and praying. Another thirty-one Quakers were confined in another building at the other end of the town.

Through the summer months the heat inside the low-ceilinged prison was quite unbearable. There was little privacy and nowhere to eat. Night and day they could hear the singing, the cursing and the clanking chains of the criminals in the cells below. The professed Quakers could be a nuisance too. Alleine himself remarked that they would bother the others

… by their cavils in the times of their preaching, praying and singing, and would come and work in their callings just by them, while they were at their duties.

Alleine and his companions took it in turns to preach and pray publicly once or twice a day. There were usually crowds from the villages around listening at the bars of the prison. The rest of the day was spent speaking to those who thronged to him for counsel and instruction. He was also allowed to curtain off a corner of the room, where he could pray in private.

After some weeks he was allowed to walk in the countryside morning and evening, if the prison keeper was in a good mood. Friends supplied him with food and money and he stayed healthy in body and mind.

On 14 July he was taken to the sessions in Taunton, where he was indicted for preaching. There was no evidence against him but he was still returned to prison. He and his companions now had to face the cold of winter, every bit as trying as the heat of summer.

It was a whole twelve months before Alleine was released again. While inside, he kept busy writing books, including an exposition of the Shorter Catechism and *A Synopsis of the Covenant*. There was a weekly letter to his people, a number of which were later collected and published under a title more associated with the later collection of John Newton, *Cardiphonia*.

He also sent out catechisms for distribution among poor families in Ilchester and nearby villages. When the jail chaplain fell ill, he dared to take his place, and, until prohibited, preached to the criminals in the jail and helped them in other ways. He was much in prayer throughout his time in prison.

Once free again, Alleine set about his work with alacrity. However, some three years on he was re-arrested, along with his wife and his aged father-in-law Richard. A further seven ministers and forty others were arrested at the same time and put in the prison in

Ilchester. Joseph Alleine was not well when he entered prison this second time and it greatly weakened him so that after returning to Taunton in February 1668, his health broke down completely. Nine months later, at the age of only thirty-four, weary from hard work and suffering, he died.

***

To take another, almost random, example, this time of a lesser-known minister, we can cite Robert Collins (1633-98), who preached in his own house in Ottery St Mary, about ten miles from Exeter in Devon, after his ejection in 1660. He testified to how one Lord's Day, in September 1670, the house was surrounded by a mob led by various officials. Not daring to break through the doors until they had a warrant, they kept the congregation prisoner until nightfall (a favourite trick, according to the historian G. R. Cragg). When the warrant arrived they forced the doors open and, on entering, treated Collins and his congregation very roughly.

They wrote down everyone's name then took some into custody, issuing warrants for two fines of £20 against Collins, the first as preacher and the second as owner of the house plus five shillings each for the hearers, though there was no proof of any illegal preaching or praying. This was followed by a great deal of breaking down doors to houses and shops, forcing gates open, taking away goods, driving off cattle and putting things on sale until the cost of the fines was more than covered.

Something similar happened again five years later and again in 1679 and yet again in 1681. On one occasion Collins was brought before a Justice of the Peace, who treated him and those with him very harshly, cursing often and calling him a minister of the devil among other terms of abuse. When Collins attempted a reply he was threatened with prison.

Then, on 25 May 1681, he and his wife were on their way to a funeral on horseback when a constable arrested them. His wife was eventually set free but Collins was taken to the constable's house and kept under guard night and day, from Wednesday to Friday, until he was brought before a magistrate. On refusing to swear the expected oath concerning the monarch's supremacy in all things ecclesiastical as well as temporal, he was sent to prison, where he remained for the next six months.

Collins was fined so often that he eventually sold his house and estate and fled to the Netherlands.

## Alehouses

As for the other part of Bunyan's statement, about the alehouse, we go again to the year 1681 and a story recorded in the memoirs of the preacher and diarist Philip Henry (1631-96), father of famous Bible commentator Matthew Henry (1662-1714). Based in Shropshire on the Welsh border, in 1658 he led the formation of the North Wales Association on the model of the Worcester Association of Richard Baxter (1615-91). Henry — neither a Separatist nor a convinced prelatist — was described by Richard Greaves as someone whose

> ... vision of non-separating nonconformity ultimately failed in 1689, but his reputation for holy living and resolute commitment to his ideals became almost legendary.

Ejected himself in October 1661, he famously wrote the following words in 1663, on what was the anniversary of the Great Ejection and of his birth:

> This day thirty two years I was born, this day twelve month I died, that fatal day to the godly painful (i.e. painstaking) faithful ministers of England amongst whom I am not worthy to be numbered.

Similar statements were made by Edward Hancock, ejected from St Philip's, Bristol, in 1662 and Devonian Nonconformist and Huguenot biographer John Quick (1636-1706), who, after ejection, carried on preaching in Brixton until arrested. Hancock spoke of being called 'to die a civil death, whilst I am naturally alive' and Quick of 'that unrighteous Act, which slew in one day two thousand able and faithful ministers of the gospel'.

The year 1681 saw a great drought in the land and a famine seemed likely. Pious people felt it time to seek the Lord and pray for disaster to be averted. In the neighbourhood where Philip Henry lived, a number agreed to set aside a day for fasting and prayer. Services were arranged at a house in Hodnet near Market Drayton, Shropshire, for 14 June 1681. On being invited to take part, Henry enquired what the situation was with regard to local Justices and was assured it would be no problem.

The writer and Nonconformist minister Edward Bury (1616-1700) of Great Bolas led in prayer as did Henry himself, before preaching on Psalm 66:18. In the middle of the sermon two Justices of the Peace suddenly arrived with others and began to speak in a very abusive and unhelpful way, shouting and swearing very loudly and harshly.

When the purpose of the meeting was explained to them, they impudently suggested that such meetings were more likely to offend God than draw down his mercy. While amusing themselves in this way, they had the names taken of all those present, about 150 altogether, then dismissed them.

In his account of the event Henry notes that

> ... the justices came to this good work from the alehouse at Prees Heath, about two miles off, to which, and to the bowling-green adjoining, they, with other justices, gentlemen and clergymen of the neighbourhood, had long before obliged themselves to come every Tuesday during the summer under a penalty of twelve pence a time if they were absent, and there to spend the day in drinking and bowling, which was thought to be as much more to the dishonour of God and the scandal of the Christian profession as cursing and swearing and drunkenness are worse than praying and singing psalms, and hearing the Word of God.

23

It would appear that the Justices knew about the meeting in Hodnet beforehand and could easily have prevented it but preferred to enjoy themselves at the expense of those present.

After they had done their work they returned to the alehouse and had further fun with their friends, going over the names taken down and remarking on some of them and recounting the whole incident to one another. It turned out that the wife of one of their number was on the list. The others thought this was very amusing and began to mock him. However, he countered by saying that she had been better employed than he and, if it was allowed, he would go a good many miles to hear Philip Henry preach. For that remark they threw him out and told him never to show his face there again. He replied that it would have been better for him and his family if such a thing had happened a long time before!

Two days later the Justices met at Hodnet again and on the word of two witnesses, no doubt sent as informers on purpose, they signed and sealed records of conviction against the house owner, who they fined £20 plus £5 because he was town constable that year; all those whose names had been taken were fined five shillings.

They also convicted Bury and Henry, even though Bury had only prayed. Praying was teaching, they claimed and they fined him £20. He could only afford £7 so they took from him his bed with the blankets and a rug, another feather bed, nineteen pairs of sheets, books to the value of £5 and some brass and pewter.

Henry was fined twice as much, £40. He refused payment so they determined to take his goods but had no right or opportunity to enter his house. Instead, therefore, they carried off more than thirty cart-loads of corn, hay, coals and other materials.

Outwardly unmoved, Henry bore it with serenity. All he would say was that it was nothing to what others were suffering or to what he himself might have to suffer in the future. He rejoiced that he was not being fined for debt or for an evil deed.

An anecdote recorded by Edmund Calamy III concerns another Puritan, Sheffield-born William Pell (1634-98). After his ejection from Great Stainton, County Durham, he was occasionally in Durham itself on the Lord's Day and once preached in a house not far from an alehouse or tavern, where, according to Calamy, some Justices of the Peace were drinking together when they 'overheard the people as they were singing a psalm'. 'Thereupon,' says Calamy,

> ... one of the company made a motion, that they should go and disturb them. To which another replied, that if any of them thought in their consciences, that singing psalms and hearing a sermon upon such a day was a more improper employment than drinking in a tavern, they might go and make them forbear; but that for his own part he would not be one of them: and so the proposition was quashed.

Pell was eventually imprisoned in Durham for Nonconformity and, following his release, ministered in various places, ending his days back in the north-east, in Newcastle.

## Strange days

Cragg says that when no magistrate was available to deal with a Dissenter or when it was not feasible to put him in a jail straight away, other arrangements had to be made. Sometimes the accused was released on parole or put under house arrest either in his own home or a house in the neighbourhood. More often, 'the prisoner was kept overnight at an alehouse or a tavern'. An example of this is recorded by Calamy with regard to Francis Bampfield (1614-84), who later became a Seventh-Day Baptist, and his curate Humphrey Philips (1632/33-1707) and their congregation in Sherborne, Dorset. There is also more than one example of this in the church book of the Baptists in Broadmead, Bristol, which notes how, in April 1682, there was a Lord's Day meeting in Upper Knowl when informers sent

… Constables and Boys from Bedminster, and would not let them meet. But it being very wet, they went after some time to an ale-house; and the while, the people met at some distance, and endured the rain.

***

Anecdotes in connection with the long period of persecution from the Great Ejection to the Toleration Act of 1689 are legion. Among the most famous are those concerning Shropshire-born Edward Lawrence (1625-95), who was ejected from Baschurch near Shrewsbury in 1662 and in 1670 was forced to move to London. Apparently, he said he had eleven good arguments against suffering by not conforming, namely a wife and ten children. When asked how he meant to maintain them all, he cheerfully replied that they 'must all live on the sixth chapter of Matthew, Take no thought for the morrow'. Sadly, one or two did not and he later wrote a book called *Parents Groans over their Wicked Children*. On the other hand, his son Nathaniel Lawrence (1670-1708) became a Nonconformist minister, serving in Banbury, Oxfordshire.

Philip Henry recalled how at grace Edward would often ask God to use his 'creatures as his witnesses that he is good' and would say 'we cannot conceive how much good our God doth every moment'. He often said, 'I adore the wisdom of God that hath not seen meet to trust me with riches.' Baxter called him a 'solid, calm, peaceable and godly man and a good Preacher'.

Another well-known anecdote, possibly legendary, is that concerning Peter Ince (1614-83), a correspondent of Baxter and a man sometimes known as the praying shepherd. In 1660 Ince was ejected from the rectory of Donhead St Mary, Wiltshire. Deprived of his living, he sought to carry on his ministry at first but eventually became a shepherd and began to work for a wealthy gentleman and Parliamentarian named Thomas Grove (1610-91) of Ferne House, Donhead St Andrew. Baxter calls him learned, humble and holy and 'of as great sincerity and integrity as almost any man I ever knew'. Some time later Grove's wife was taken dangerously ill. When the parish minister was called for to pray with her he sent back word that he was about to go hunting with hounds and would come only when the hunt was over.

Grove was understandably upset with the man's attitude and said so. A servant overhearing him spoke up and said, 'Sir, our shepherd, if you will send for him, can pray, very well; we have often heard him at prayer in the field.' On hearing this, Grove sent for immediately for Ince. When he arrived Ince was asked whether he could pray. Looking intently at Grove, he replied, 'God forbid, sir, I should live one day without prayer'.

Being asked then to pray with the sick lady, he did so with great fluency and fervency so that all present were quite astonished. When they rose from their knees, Grove spoke up and asked for his story. Ince explained his situation and in reply Grove said that from now on Ince should be 'my shepherd'. A meeting-house was soon erected on the estate and Ince preached there regularly to a gathered church of Dissenters.

Ince is said to have been a good scholar, skilled in Hebrew, and a preacher whose sermons were always full of application. He was especially gifted at public prayer, and would, on days of special prayer, 'pour forth his soul with such spirituality, variety, fluency and affection' that he was known as *Praying Ince*.

In 1662 Ince was imprisoned for eighteen months in Dorchester with several others, after they had preached in Shaftesbury. At first they refused to give assurances of their future good behaviour but for the sake of friends and family, they all eventually did except for Bampfield, who remained defiant and was only freed ten years later. Ince was again brought before the quarter sessions in 1676 for Nonconformist preaching.

\*\*\*

What days they were, that period from 1660 to 1689. They were indeed days when those who pleaded for the Spirit of prayer could often be found in prison and when those who opposed them were often found in the alehouse. It is the detail of what happened in this period of time and why these things happened that we wish to explore in this book.

# 2 | THE HOTTER SORT OF PROTESTANT — THE MORE REMOTE BACKGROUND TO 1662

In order to consider the Great Ejection of 1662 it will be useful to start somewhere further back. In his 1962 lecture, Dr Lloyd-Jones, waxing lyrical, described 1662 as a river estuary. To properly understand a river, he said, you need to trace it to its source in the hills, as it were. A hundred years earlier, in 1861, Charles Stanford used a similar image, that of springs and outfalls.

We can think too of a journey's beginning and end, an arrow's flight from bow to target or the image of a Bible text, which we can only understand if we know its context, especially what has gone before. To properly tell the story of the Great Ejection, we need first to briefly trace about 150 years of English history leading up to this momentous event and the origins of Puritanism.

## The Tudors

It was in the sixteenth century that the great movement of God known as the Reformation swept across Europe. Through Martin Luther (1483-1546) and others, attention was drawn again to fundamental but forgotten truths such as justification by faith and the sufficiency of Scripture. England was ruled over at that time by the Tudors, whose dynasty begins with Henry Tudor. Following his victory at Bosworth Field in 1485, he was crowned Henry VII.

### *Henry VIII*

On his father's death in 1509, Henry VIII ascended to the throne. It was during his reign that the far-reaching religious, social and political changes associated with the Reformation first came to England. Henry himself warmed to Reformers like Thomas Cranmer (1489-1556) but was unsympathetic to many aspects of the movement. In 1521 Pope Leo X famously made him Defender of the Faith in recognition of his anti-Lutheran treatise defending the seven sacraments of Rome.

In 1532 England repudiated the Pope's authority and Henry became Supreme Head (later Governor) of the Church of England. It is suggested that some of Henry's queens, Anne Boleyn (*c.* 1504-36) and Catherine Parr (1512-48) especially, were sympathetic to the Reformation. Henry, however, like many others in England, remained a Roman Catholic at heart.

### *Edward VI and Mary*

Henry died in 1547 and was succeeded by his nine-year-old son, Edward, who had a decidedly Protestant upbringing. When he ascended to the throne many good people saw him as a new Josiah who, through the regency council appointed by his father, would lead the nation into a glorious new Protestant age.

In fact, unlike Josiah, the boy king reigned less than six years and when his sister Mary succeeded him she did her utmost to throw into reverse all the advances of the previous reign. For the five years Bloody Mary ruled she sought to turn England back to its old Romanist ways, burning at the stake men like Cranmer, Nicholas Ridley (*c.* 1500-55) and around 300 other Protestant martyrs. Hundreds more fled to the Continent, men like Scots Reformer John Knox (*c.* 1514-72) and the author of *Foxe's Book of Martyrs*, John Foxe (1517-87).

### Elizabeth

In 1558, Mary was in turn succeeded by her sister Elizabeth. Many had seen what they felt was a better sort of Protestantism on the Continent in men such as John Calvin (1509-64) and Henry Bullinger (1504-75) and hoped Elizabeth would bring in further Protestant reforms.

However, she saw it as her duty to steer more of a middle course, away from the extremism of the previous reign yet not too much in the direction desired by men like Knox and Foxe. This meant that though Protestantism was allowed to flourish to some extent during her forty-five-year-long reign, more radical Protestants were suppressed and unresolved tensions and frustrations were allowed to grow. It was, as Robert Bosher and others have pointed out 'a peculiarly English expression' of the Reformation.

## The Puritans

'If we are to understand 1662,' Lloyd-Jones cautions, 'we must understand the real and essential nature of Puritanism'. Men like the Marian martyrs Ridley, Cranmer, Hugh Latimer (*c.* 1487-1555) and John Hooper (*c.* 1495-1555) exhibited a Puritan spirit even in Henry VIII's time. By the time of Elizabeth we see the rise of the Puritan movement itself with men like William Whitaker (1548-95) and William Perkins (1558-1602) being very influential.

Carl Trueman is not the first to have observed that the word Puritan 'has proved notoriously difficult to define'. He says, help-fully, that 'it remains true to say that it is easier to give examples of Puritans than give a precise and fully adequate definition'. In differing contexts the word can have different cultural, political and religious overtones.

Puritans were, however, clearly a 'hotter sort of Protestant', as someone put it at the time. In the twentieth century Ernest Kevan suggested we should understand Puritanism 'first, as the endeavour to effect thoroughgoing reforms of ecclesiastical practice, and second, as the attempt at a godly way of life'. Puritans wanted to see Romanist barnacles from the Middle Ages scraped away both from the church and from people's hearts and for the Reformation to be completed. They longed for a church pure in practice as well as in doctrine. Their fundamental idea was, according to nineteenth-century writer John Brown,

> ... the supreme authority of Scripture brought to bear upon the conscience as opposed to an unenlightened reliance on the priesthood and the outward ordinances of the Church.

Puritans seemed, to themselves at least, he says, to be aiming not at singularity,

> ... but at obedience to that higher spiritual order prevailing in the universe, which he recognised as being the expression of the mind of God, and therefore of more commanding authority than the mere arrangements and requirements of man.

Brown instances reverence for Scripture, belief in God's sovereign majesty, a severe morality, popular sympathies and fervent attachment to the cause of civil freedom as typical of the Puritan spirit.

It can be argued that such opposition to Elizabeth's so-called *via media*, to which she became increasingly attached as her long reign wore on, was eventually bound to put them at loggerheads with less radical people and lead, ultimately, even though it was not what the majority had in mind, to the sort of Nonconformity that existed from 1662 onwards.

In Elizabeth's reign both Romanists and Puritans suffered for Nonconformity. In 1593 there was both an act forbidding recusants (Romanists who refused to attend the parish church) to move more than five miles from their homes and another act mandating prison without bail for anyone over sixteen who failed to attend the parish church, persuaded others to do the same, denied her Majesty's authority in matters ecclesiastical or attended unlawful religious conventicles. Such a crime could lead to punishment for the guilty and even exile for those who persisted in their obstinacy. This was the law that in Charles II's time was used against Bunyan and others.

In Elizabeth's own time the influential and impulsive Thomas Cartwright (*c.* 1535-1603) wanted to see the national church governed in a Presbyterian way rather than the episcopal way it was — that is, under bishops — and for such advocacy suffered imprisonment and exile. Growing numbers of people tried to serve God outside the confines of the national church and also suffered. Such people often sought, in the famous words of the volatile Robert Browne (1550-1633), 'reformation without tarrying for any'. In 1581 Browne and Robert Harrison (d. 1585), gathered a Separatist church in Norwich that was forced into exile. Similarly, in the 1590s, John Greenwood and Henry Barrowe attempted something similar and were hanged at Tyburn for it in 1593. Meanwhile on the Continent many so-called 'semi-separatists' could be found who gathered churches without wholly giving up the idea of a national church, men such as Henry Jacob (1563-1624) and William Bradshaw (1571-1618).

## James I

Elizabeth was the last of the Tudors. The Virgin Queen was succeeded, on her death in 1603, by James VI of Scotland, who at that point also became James I of England, being a descendant of Henry VII through his daughter Margaret.

Given the new king's Scots Presbyterian background, some hoped, as in Edward's time, that he would usher in a new Protestant era but

James loathed his Presbyterian upbringing and was very much drawn to episcopal church government, government by bishops. On coming south his motto appears to have become 'No bishop, no king'.

Remembered best now for his role in initiating the King James Bible, he early set about imposing conformity on the church over which, like his Tudor predecessors, he was Supreme Governor. He is reported to have said of the Puritans at the famous Hampton Court Conference, 'I'll make them conform, or I'll harry them out of this land, or else do worse.' One famous battle with the Puritans was over the 'Book of Sports', which commended Sunday archery, dancing and jumping games, though it placed bowls and bear-baiting off limits. James commanded all Anglican ministers to announce these guidelines to their congregations though he was resisted by his archbishop George Abbot (1562-1633) and by the strictly sabbatarian Puritans. Another feature of James's reign was the growth of the modified Calvinism known as Arminianism that had begun on the Continent just after his accession.

In this climate a significant number of Puritans again voted with their feet and headed for the Continent. A famous example of the Separatist trend in James's reign concerns the church originally gathered in Scrooby, Nottinghamshire, under the leadership of Richard Clyfton (d. 1616), John Robinson (1575-1625) and others. Persecution forced them to emigrate, like others, first to the Netherlands in 1608 and then, after a peaceful few years, they eventually left Plymouth, England, for America in the *Mayflower* in 1620. It was another of their leaders, William Bradford (1590-1657), who later spoke of them as 'pilgrims and strangers upon the earth', giving rise to the term 'Pilgrim Fathers'.

Having endured a horrific voyage across the Atlantic, they then suffered a cruel winter, fever, fires, accidents and the arrival of ungodly settlers. Within six months half the original party of 120 had died but, by prayer and providence, the rest survived and in 1630 the remainder of the Leyden congregation joined them. The settlement soon reached 300 in number. Their history is part of a story we cannot pursue here, that of New England and America.

## Charles I

Charles I succeeded his father in 1625 and with his Archbishop of Canterbury from 1633, William Laud (1573-1645), he determined to continue and intensify the policy of imposing on the national church conformity to the Book of Common Prayer. Laud also opposed Calvinistic doctrine and Puritan piety and savage persecution was unleashed on men like Scots Puritan Alexander Leighton (1587-*c*. 1644) and English Puritan William Prynne (1600-69) who were both branded and had their ears cropped.

In 1637 Laud tried to impose episcopacy and the Prayer Book on Scotland and ran into big trouble. In Edinburgh doughty Jenny Geddes famously resisted its public reading by throwing a stool at the Dean's head! 'Will ye dare read that book in my lug?' she enquired. The Bishops' Wars between England and Scotland ensued, the Scots uniting under the renewed Scots national covenant of 1638, forerunner to the Solemn League and Covenant of 1643. Then, in 1640, what was called the '*Etcetera* Oath' was introduced, an oath which, while denouncing Romanism, required ministers and others to pledge themselves to upholding episcopacy and the Anglican hierarchy of the day in these words '… nor will I ever give my consent to alter the government of this Church by archbishops, bishops, deans, and archdeacons, *etcetera*, as it stands now established, and as by right it ought to stand…'

Meanwhile, in New England, the number of colonists eager to escape persecution and establish churches had reached 20,000. A form of Nonconformity was soon well established. Back on this side of the water, men like William Wroth (1576-1642), deprived of his living in Monmouthshire, were gathering churches 'according to the New England pattern', that is as Independent churches.

Both inside and outside the established church, those who wanted to follow what they saw as more biblical patterns were often finding it tough under Laud. It can be argued that his policies drove Puritans towards Separatism. Certainly, they contributed to the resistance to the king from Parliament that led to the series of wars that became known as the Wars of the Three Kingdoms, beginning with the Bishops' Wars in 1639 and 1640 and culminating in the Third English Civil War of 1650 and 1651.

## Oliver Cromwell

As Parliament gained ascendancy over the king, episcopacy was abolished in England and use of the Common Book of Prayer officially prohibited, though it quietly persisted within some quarters. In 1648 General Thomas Pride (d. 1658) at the head of the Independent-dominated New Model Army purged the Presbyterian-dominated Long Parliament of 200 of its MPs. Soon, the House of Lords and the monarchy were abolished and on 30 January 1649, Charles I was beheaded. First under the Commonwealth then, from 1653, under the Protectorate of Oliver Cromwell relief came to the Puritans and previously marginalized religionists of many shades.

In 1654 many Church of England ministers were removed from their parishes or sequestered by Cromwell's famous Triers, a group of thirty-eight men appointed to root out incumbents, chiefly where there was evidence of inefficiency, incompetence, immorality or heresy, though some were removed, it has to be said, for using the Prayer Book too frequently and other unpopular acts.

It was during this period, 1643-49, that the famous Westminster Assembly sat, by government request. It failed to bring about the intended Reformed alliance between England and Scotland but it produced documents, such as the Westminster Confession and the Larger and Shorter Catechisms, that are among the finest theological productions ever penned.

Some Assembly members were convinced Anglicans. Most were Presbyterian, Presbyterianism being increasingly in the ascendancy at this time. Their leaders published a book in 1641 under the unlikely name of Smectymnuus, an acronym for Stephen Marshall (c. 1594-1655), Edmund Calamy (1600-66), a Scotsman called

Thomas Young (1587-1655), Matthew Newcomen (1610-69) and William Spurstowe (*c.* 1605-66).

Some few were Independents or Congregationalists. Known as the Dissenting Brethren, these men included Thomas Goodwin (1600-80) and Jeremiah Burroughs (*c.* 1600-46). There was some debate among this group about nomenclature. Men like John Cotton (1585-1662), invited to the Assembly though in America by this time, preferred Congregationalist to Independent. Such men certainly wanted to distance themselves from the Separatists of the time.

In 1655 Baxter prepared his famous *Reformed Pastor* for the first meeting of the Worcestershire Association of churches. Baxter saw looser associations such as these united 'in the practice of so much of discipline as the Episcopal, Presbyterians and Independents are agreed in, and as crosseth none of their principles' as the way forward. Several other county associations were formed in this period.

## The Bedford Baptists

The Particular or Calvinistic Baptists were not represented at Westminster but are an example of various more or less orthodox groups emerging at this time. In 1644 they had at least seven congregations in England. By 1660 there were 130 such churches, as well as 110 General or Arminian Baptist churches. Some of these Baptist churches excluded non-Baptists, others were more open.

In 1650 a famous Independent and Baptist church was established in Bedford. With just twelve members at first, it was led by John Gifford (d. 1655). From 1653, when the Anglican vicar was deposed, this congregation, now with twenty-five members, met in the parish church, as did new Independent congregations elsewhere.

The Bedford church's most famous member would be then newly converted John Bunyan. He would eventually become their pastor.

Bunyan began to preach around the time Gifford died. He was soon set aside for this work but continued in his 'tinkering' trade too. By this point membership had grown to around ninety and the church was enjoying great peace. In 1660, however, all this would come to an end, not only in Bedford but in many other places too.

## Sects and parties

At this time England was swamped by a multitude of sects and parties. In his *Gangraena* of 1646 Thomas Edwards (1599-1647) identified some sixteen sects and more than 175 errorists. Given his contention that Independency was 'mother, nurse and patroness of all other errors', we must allow for overstatement. However, there were many heresies, including the millenarian Fifth Monarchists, a movement that would end with a rising led by Thomas Venner in 1661; various antinomians, including the short-lived Ranters and the Grindletonians and Muggletonians; the anti-Trinitarian Socinians and the Seekers, who were precursors of the Quakers.

The Quakers, or Society of Friends, were a group with no official creed but which was characterized by a quiet mysticism. They were widely persecuted both before and after the Restoration, chiefly because of their refusal to take oaths. 'Poor deluded souls' Baxter called them. Their leader was George Fox (1624-91). Fox and over two thousand others were imprisoned in the Interregnum and about thirty died in prison. One of the most notorious Quakers was James Nayler (1618-80). In 1656 he rode into Bristol in a blasphemous re-enactment of Palm Sunday, for which he was pilloried, whipped through the streets, branded on his forehead and pierced with a red-hot iron through his tongue. He was then given three years' solitary confinement with hard labour.

Besides these religious groups there were also more political ones like the Levellers and Diggers who sought greater equality for working men.

## Richard Cromwell

In September 1658 Oliver Cromwell unexpectedly died and was succeeded by his son, Richard, who, as one writer puts it, 'had neither the genius for government nor the moral enthusiasm of his father' nor, adds Michael Watts, 'his father's sense of divine calling nor the confidence of the army'. And so he soon 'retired in disgust from the control of men and affairs'.

With Richard's abdication in May 1659 the country returned briefly to its Commonwealth rather than Protectorate status but with the unopposed arrival in the capital the following February of General George Monck (1608-70) and his Scots army, the Long Parliament was finally dissolved and a new Convention Parliament called — that is, one not summoned by a monarch. Within a week they had agreed to recall Charles as king by recognising his reign to have begun with the death of his father in January 1649.

The latter years of the Interregnum were uncertain times and after Cromwell's death many feared anarchy. We need to bear this in mind if we are to understand why, having rid itself of one King Charles, the nation was so eager — just over ten years years later — to replace him with another.

Of course, there were always those who hankered after a king. In 1651 Christopher Love (1618-51) had been executed for his part in a plot to restore the monarchy. It was not the only one. As far as they were concerned, the Republican experiment had utterly failed. Many were fed up with the restrictions that prohibited entertainments such as stage plays and horse racing.

Others had never been great advocates of republicanism and simply felt that true religion was as likely to thrive under a king as under a protector. They had accepted Cromwell's leadership, in Stanford's words, 'not as the best in itself, but as the best the case would allow'. Stanford quotes Edward Pearse (1631-94) in his *Conformists Plea for the Nonconformists*, who says of the Presbyterians that they cannot drink the king's health but 'they helpt to pray him to his throne'. Baxter was typical of Presbyterians when he wrote:

> We are bound by the covenant to the king that last was; and by the oath of allegiance, to him and his heirs; and all changes since have been made unlawfully by rebellious sectaries; and for our parts, whatever others have done, we have taken no engagements or contrary oaths: Therefore, being obliged to the king as the undoubted heir of the crown, we ought to do our duty as loyal subjects to restore him, and for the issue let God do what he will.

It was generally felt that royalty had been taught its lesson and the failures leading up to the beheading of Charles I would surely not be repeated by his son if he became king.

*\*\*\**

Thus we see the rise of Puritanism chiefly within but also in some cases without the established church and something of the fluctuations in their cause under various regimes prior to the beginning of the reign of Charles II. Things had been difficult under Elizabeth and the earlier Stuarts and much easier after the execution of Charles I. Though many did not see it at first, with the return of the monarchy things were about to get much more difficult indeed.

# 3 | AN END TO THE PURITAN DREAM — 1662 AND THE IMMEDIATE BACKGROUND

The Restoration is the shorthand term used to describe the restoring of the combined English, Scottish and Irish monarchy to the rightful heir, Charles Stuart, in 1660, following the Interregnum that succeeded the Wars of the Three Kingdoms. The term can apply both to the actual event or the period immediately following.

In the nineteenth century John Stoughton wrote that the Restoration was accomplished by treachery and intrigue so that

> ... after years of war and suffering for the sake of liberty, the people were seen prostrate at the feet of Charles II; asking no guarantees against the revival of despotism, but rather craving forgiveness for the victories they had won.

It was on 25 May 1660 that King Charles arrived in Dover. By the time of his thirtieth birthday, four days later, he was in London. News of his coming preceded him. Church bells rang and the streets of Merry England thronged with rejoicing people marking the event with banners and oak boughs and bonfires. The king had come 'to enjoy his own again'! News travelled slowly in those days and it was a few weeks before some people realized what was happening but eventually the news ran to every corner of these islands.

What nineteenth-century Scots minister Thomas M'Crie called a 'Lent of twenty years' was about to be succeeded by 'a carnival of licentious revelry'. The Puritan vision of a godly reformation for England had all come to nothing, it seemed. True religion was at a very low ebb indeed.

## The main parties at the time of the Restoration

Apart from the Quakers and other fringe groups mentioned in the last chapter, there were, broadly speaking, four main religious groups in existence in England by 1660. The first two were largely excluded from the discussions that began at this time.

### Romanists

At one extreme were those who, like the Giffard family in Staffordshire or the Arundells in Wiltshire, remained Roman Catholic. In some places these were in the majority. They had been assured of Charles's sympathies. He had long been rumoured to be a Romanist but for understandable reasons kept this quiet, only converting on his deathbed. No doubt the Romanists were more optimistic about their prospects than they had been previously, even if they had no opportunity to openly express such sentiments.

### Congregationalists

At the other extreme were the Congregationalists, both within and without the established church. Outside you had Baptists such as Bunyan and William Kiffin (1616-1701). Within the established church you had men such as Westminster Divines Burroughs and

Goodwin, who we have already mentioned. The greatest of the Independents was undoubtedly John Owen (1616-83), dubbed by a contemporary 'the Calvin of England'. He became convinced of Congregationalism in the 1640s reading Cotton's *Keys of the Kingdom.*

Thanks to Cromwell's sympathy, this group had begun to grow from around 1553, as had the other more radical religious and political sects. The tide had now turned against them and their prospects were not good. Opportunities for being heard were very small indeed. Richard Baxter says that they told the king 'all that they desired was … to hold their own liberty of worship and discipline, in sole dependence on the king'. They sought toleration by the church rather than comprehension within it.

### Presbyterians

Most Puritans by this time were Presbyterians, though the term was used in quite a loose way in England, as opposed to Scotland. English Presbyterians were non-episcopal and did not consider the Prayer Book necessary. Leaders included Baxter, Edmund Calamy the elder, Edward Reynolds (1599-1676) and Thomas Manton (1620-77). Calamy was a Westminster Divine, and Manton, whose voluminous writings continue to be in print, was a secretary to the Assembly. Both were among Cromwell's Triers but opposed to the execution of Charles I. Manton's voluminous writings continue to be in print.

While happy to be ruled over in the state by a king, the Presbyterians were opposed to bishops in the church. They had prospered in the late 1540s and early 1550s and at the beginning of the Restoration were hopeful that the tide was with them. They sought comprehension within the Church of England.

### Episcopalians

In the driving seat, however, were those who had remained faithful to the old order through the hard and unpromising years when there was no king. Some, like James Ussher (1581-1656), Archbishop of Armagh, and Jeremy Taylor (1613-67), had been ejected by Cromwell's Triers. Others had simply kept quiet.

Such formalists often held Puritanism in contempt and hated Presbyterianism. Royalist to a man, they rejoiced in the Restoration and many saw in it an opportunity to reassert themselves and their ideas afresh.

## What the Presbyterians wanted

Millard outlines Presbyterian demands under four headings:

- *Limitation of the scope and powers of the episcopal office.* Most were happy enough for a bishop to preside over a board of ministers but not as by divine right. They wanted more suffragan or assistant bishops and for power to be devolved to local pastors.

- *A more thorough and effective system of spiritual discipline.* They wanted church membership to reflect spiritual reality much more than it did under the parish system, where everyone was assumed to be a Christian.

- *Omission of certain ceremonial acts and prohibition of certain vestments,* as outlined elsewhere in this chapter.

- *Thorough revision of the Prayer Book.* They sought alterations, omissions and additions. They believed that although there may have been an argument for avoiding too much change in the transition period to the new religion, it was now high time that the book was stripped of all lingering Romanist remnants. They also wanted extempore prayer to be allowed and for a minister to be free to omit parts of the liturgy as he saw fit. They wanted all the readings to be from Scripture and not to include the Apocrypha. They were also unhappy about the way people were assumed to be Christians, some of the terminology and certain obsolete words. They also wanted the psalter to be improved.

The changes they desired were many but these men were not Separatists. They remained in full sympathy with the idea of a comprehensive and established national church. What they wanted was a church that was broad enough to include all who were reasonable and moderate.

## What the Episcopalians wanted

Contrary to Presbyterian hopes, it was the assumption of the Episcopalians that the king's restoration would lead to a return, ecclesiastically, to the situation that existed before Charles was beheaded. Ultimately, they refused to accept any other idea. Some were also bent on a measure of revenge, though they proceeded with caution so as not to divulge the extremes to which they were willing to go to have their way enforced.

## The Declaration of Breda

In the period while negotiations for a restoration were afoot, several Presbyterian ministers travelled to the Continent, where they gained the impression that Charles was very pious, fit to be a fine king and one who would do no harm to their cause. A story circulated that he had been overheard praying in a very meek manner by a deputation that met him in the Hague. The story made the Presbyterian Thomas Case (1598-1692) lift his hands to God in thanksgiving. Case was the longest-surviving Westminster Divine to be ejected. He had tried to bring Charles back in 1651. At his funeral he was described as 'a scriptural preacher; a great man in prayer, and one who brought home many souls to God'.

The perception of Charles as one who would benefit the cause proved to be misleading to say the least. Even at the time there were doubters. Thomas Crosby's *History of the Baptists* refers to Daniel Dyke (1614-88) as one who 'foresaw the storm that was coming, and the snares that must attend a man of his principles' if he remained in the established church and so resigned his living in 1660. An articulate man of exceptional integrity he had been another of Cromwell's Triers. When Case tried to convince him of their rosy prospects,

Dyke told his friend plainly that such hopes were deceptive. Even if the king himself proved true, those around him would have other ideas and would 'in all probability not only turn them out, but take away their liberty too', which is just what happened.

The Presbyterian idea was that if a 'reduced episcopacy' and a 'reformed liturgy' could be introduced, everyone would be happy. They were encouraged to be positive about Charles by the Declaration of Breda, issued the month previous to his restoration. The declaration granted a general pardon to all subjects who should lay hold of it within forty days, unless excepted by Parliament.

The Indemnity and Oblivion Act, which had its first and second readings before Charles's return, became law at the end of August 1660. Crown lands and those of the established church were automatically restored but property was not returned to all Royalists or others who had opposed the Cromwellian regime. Many were officially pardoned, including *Paradise Lost* author, John Milton (1608-74), who was released from prison.

Parliament eventually excepted only some fifty from the Indemnity Act. These were executed or imprisoned chiefly for their role in the death of the previous king. By 1660 some thirty-one of the fifty-nine who signed the death warrant were still alive. Several of these fled to New England or the Continent. Others were executed. One of those hanged, drawn and quartered was the Fifth Monarchist Thomas Harrison (1606-60). Another was the preacher Hugh Peter (1598-1660). As C. R. Cragg says:

> ... a few notable Puritans were left in doubt as to their status, and feared for their lives as well as for their liberty, but on the whole the great upheaval was accomplished at a singularly modest price in blood.

The Declaration of Breda included the statement that

> Because the passion and uncharitableness of the times have produced several opinions in religion, by which men are engaged

in parties and animosities against each other ... we do declare a liberty to tender consciences, and that no man shall be disquieted or called in question for differences of opinion in matter of religion, which do not disturb the peace of the kingdom; and that we shall be ready to consent to such an Act of Parliament, as, upon mature deliberation, shall be offered to us, for the full granting that indulgence.

Charles made many such conciliatory noises at first but his new parliament would soon insist on restoring all the old forms and ceremonies of the church. 'The opening of the new reign was a morning full of promise,' says Stanford, 'but after a few hours, threatening clouds began to gather'.

There is some debate over what really went on in the opening years of Charles's reign. Were he and his government just biding their time before they struck? Or is it true to say, as I. M. Green argues, that in that period 'Charles II did all that he could to bring about a compromise settlement of the church'? Gerald Bray says that it seems

... the king himself was sincere enough in his statements but he was surrounded by men who were thirsting for revenge. Once he was safely back on the throne, Charles found that he had to make concessions to these extremists, and the good intentions of Breda were seriously compromised as a result.

Beside the revenge motive, there was a fear that the events of 1642 would be repeated.

Michael Watts posits that Charles was either a jaded and worldly sceptic who looked on all religions with tolerant indifference or, more coherently, a sincere but secret Roman Catholic doing his best to win toleration for his fellow religionists. The truth is that we cannot be sure what Charles had in mind. The facts are, however, that after a relatively short honeymoon period of less than two years the events that led directly to the Great Ejection of 1662 were set in motion.

## The early months of the Restoration

When Charles arrived in London the faithful old Puritan Arthur Jackson (*c.* 1593-1666), a veteran of Love's 1651 plot, presented him with a richly-bound Bible, which Charles, ironically as it would turn out, promised would be the rule of his actions. About a dozen Puritans, including Baxter, Reynolds, Calamy, Manton and the scholarly preacher William Bates (1625-90), were made court chaplains. Some of them actually preached to Charles, including Baxter, who apparently gave a very long sermon without 'one courtly phrase to relieve his censure of the vices of the great'.

Less than a month after his arrival Charles received a delegation presented by the Lord Chamberlain, Lord Manchester, Edward Montagu (1602-71). The delegation was led by Reynolds, Calamy and Baxter, who stressed the importance of union between different factions within the national church. Differences among the various parties, they said, were over liturgy and ceremony, church government and discipline, not 'the doctrinal truths of the reformed religion'. They felt union could be procured if only what was necessary to communion was insisted on, if discipline against sin was enforced and if faithful ministers were not replaced by unworthy ones.

The issue was not the existence of a state church, royal supremacy in ecclesiastical matters or the use of liturgy but, as the king saw, the problem of church government. Charles asked how much they were willing to concede. They felt they were unable to speak for all ministers but, after consultations at Sion College, they floated the idea of a moderated episcopacy. They spoke of the scheme drawn up by Ussher, which Baxter called a 'reduction of episcopacy to the form of synodical government received in the ancient church' and that involved smaller dioceses, more bishops and the bishop consulting his presbyters.

The Presbyterians also wanted the Book of Common Prayer revised by 'learned, godly and moderate divines'. Distancing themselves from Owen's view that written prayers were unacceptable they argued only for something more biblical that would not be enforced too rigidly and that would allow for extempore prayers.

As we shall see, they also objected to things like wearing the surplice, baptizing with the sign of the cross, using a ring in marriage services, bowing at altars and at the name of Jesus, kneeling at the Lord's Supper and observing saints' days — all vestiges of Romanism that they wanted to see abolished or at least not insisted on. They argued that change is good in the case of 'things indifferent', in Calvin's words, 'lest they should, by perpetual permanency and constant use, be judged by the people as necessary as the substantial of worship'.

Charles cautiously expressed willingness to seek what the Presbyterians sought but when pressed he was unwilling to make a public commitment. Baxter wrote that on hearing of Charles's zeal to search for peaceful compromise between the religious parties 'old Mr. Ash burst out into tears with joy and could not forbear expressing what gladness this promise of his majesty had put into his heart'. This was Westminster Divine Simeon Ashe, who, Baxter tells us, would later refuse to conform and 'was buried on the eve of Bartholomew Day'.

Despite the Presbyterians' high hopes of inclusion in the established church and the royal assurances they received that respect would be paid to their conscientious scruples, all was not well. Their opponents had no intention of compromising but were determined to remove the Puritans, root and branch, from the national church. Once the bishops discovered what the Presbyterians proposed they objected 'with speed and emphasis' says nineteenth-century Scots writer Peter Bayne They scoffed at the emphasis on regular ministry, more informal fellowship and honouring the Sabbath day. They rejected such low views of episcopacy, praised the Prayer Book, decried extempore prayer and defended church ceremonial to the hilt.

Baxter did prepare a reply to the bishops in which he wondered if they understood anything about conscience at all. Have they 'resolved to send all the honest men among us out of the country, if not out of the world?' he wonders. 'Be it known to you, however,' he adds 'come what may, the man who is true to his God and his conscience will not do that which he taketh to be sin.' At the time it was felt by others that Baxter's reply would only inflame the situation and not do any good, so it was kept private.

## The Act for Confirming and Restoring Ministers

In September the Act for Confirming and Restoring of Ministers was passed. This was intended to deal with the perceived problem of ministers who had been sequestered in Cromwell's time. As stated, most such sequestered men were utterly unworthy of their office. They were removed because they were incompetent or immoral, though at times men were removed because of their Royalist sympathies, as in the cases of men like Ussher and Taylor.

This new act was not concerned with keeping out illiterates or drunkards but stated that

> Every sequestered minister who has not justified the late King's murder, or declared against infant baptism, shall be restored to his living before the 25th of December next ensuing, and the present incumbent shall peaceably quit it, and be accountable for dilapidations, and all arrears of fifths not paid.

This act ejected hundreds of good men from their livings, including Thomas Goodwin. A. G. Matthews calculated that a total of 695, mostly Puritan, ministers were ejected but suggests that some fifty-nine of these were able to find livings again before falling foul of the Act of Uniformity two years later. Watts points out that even before this some fifty Congregationalist ministers had voluntarily withdrawn from the vicarages they had occupied during the Republic. Among those restored were people like the vicar of Bedford, which meant that the Baptist congregation mentioned in the previous chapter had to leave the parish church.

R. S. Bosher contentiously calls it 'a Presbyterian measure making certain concessions to Anglicans, rather than vice-versa'. Certainly, the only people explicitly excluded were Republicans and Baptists.

## The Worcester House Declaration

In October 1660, Charles made the Worcester House Declaration, — a declaration which, to the surprise even of the most optimistic Presbyterians, gave them almost everything they were asking for. Despite this, Baxter — still not fully aware of where things were headed — had suggestions for further modifications.

The declaration promised no peremptory insistence on cere-monies, the continuance of a moderated episcopacy, respect for the Lord's Day and the removal of incompetent, negligent or immoral clergy. Suffragan bishops would be appointed in every diocese. Admittance to the Lord's Table would be on profession of faith. Revision of the Book of Common Prayer would be considered.

A promised conference at Worcester House followed, involving on one side, Gilbert Sheldon (1598-1677), the new Bishop of London, who would become Archbishop of Canterbury in 1663; Humphrey Henchman (1592-1675), Sheldon's successor in the capital but then Bishop of Salisbury; George Morley (1597-1684), Bishop of Worcester; John Cosin (1594-1672), Bishop of Durham; John Gauden (1605-82), later Bishop of Exeter; John Hacket (1592-1670), Bishop of Coventry; John Barwick (1612-64), Dean of St Paul's; the Cambridge academic Peter Gunning (1614-84) and many others plus noblemen. On the other were Reynolds, Calamy, Ashe, Manton, Spurstowe and Baxter.

It was at this conference that the idea of allowing the Independents certain freedoms in a religious settlement was raised. The Presbyterians feared that this was an excuse to raise the spectre of toleration for Romanists and so opposed the idea. Thus divided, the Puritans were easier prey.

So things looked good. Reynolds accepted the title of Bishop of Norwich. Baxter and Calamy chose to wait before accepting the bishoprics offered to them. When the declaration actually came before Parliament to be ratified at the end of November 1660, however, the House rejected it. It has been suggested that they acted on the advice of the king, though it cannot be proved.

## Venner's Rising

In January 1661 there was a rising led by Thomas Venner, a wine cooper and Fifth Monarchist. Venner had led an armed rising against Cromwell in 1657 but his life was spared. The 1661 rising was a reaction to the way the new regime had treated Thomas Harrison. Venner and about fifty others terrorized the City of London for three days, entering the old St Paul's and killing more than twenty people until repulsed by the king's lifeguards and a force of General Monck's men. Some were shot where they stood and Venner was captured after being badly wounded. He was tried at the Old Bailey then, like Harrison the previous year, hanged, drawn and quartered.

This event created a stir among those who believed republicanism to be far from dead. In a matter of days the government had banned meetings of 'Anabaptists, Quakers and Fifth Monarchy men' and in a matter of weeks more than four thousand Quakers were imprisoned. Soon Baptists were also being dragged from their beds and Newgate Prison alone held 289 of these and others arrested at unlawful meetings.

## The Savoy Conference

Shortly before Charles's official coronation, in April 1661, a conference commenced at the Savoy in London's Strand. The duration of the conference was limited to four months from the date of its commission (25 March). At the end of this period, the result was to be reported to the king in writing. Ostensibly, the conference was intended to discuss ways of bringing about reconciliation between opposing factions within the Church. In reality, the issues had already been decided.

The conference was convened by Sheldon. The London venue was his lodgings at the Savoy. The original Savoy, a beautiful building named for Peter, Duke of Savoy, uncle to Henry III's Queen Eleanor, was destroyed by Wat Tyler's rebels in 1381 and replaced by a humbler building that was first a monastery, then an almshouse, a hospital and at last a dwelling place.

Lee Gatiss calls Sheldon 'a royalist anglican of the first rank'. 'An admirable representative of the school of high and dry Churchmen', says Bayne. He had been imprisoned in the 1640s by order of Parliament and was intimate with Royalist leaders in the Civil War period, ministering to Charles I in captivity and collecting funds for Charles II during his exile. Cragg calls him 'an ecclesiastic, not a theologian' and a bitter opponent of Calvinism wherever it appeared. As Bishop of London, Gatiss says, he was charged with reimposing order and uniformity on a diverse and radicalized diocese and was not afraid to use strong-arm tactics to achieve his end.

Some twenty-four commissioners attended the Savoy Conference. On one side were Sheldon; the nominal chairman, Accepted Frewen (1588-1664), Archbishop of York; also Henchman, Morley and eight more bishops. On the other side were twelve representative Presbyterian ministers led by Reynolds, who later conformed as did John Conant (1608-94), Reynolds' son-in-law; and John Wallis (1616-1703). The other nine all became Dissenters — Baxter; Calamy; Case; Jackson; Manton; Newcomen; the later biographer Samuel Clarke (1599-1682); the former head of Emmanuel College, Cambridge Anthony Tuckney (1599-1670); and 'ancient, calm, reverend' William Spurstowe (whose widow married Tuckney in 1668).

Each side also had nine assistants or coadjutors. The Presbyterians included John Lightfoot (1602-75), who later conformed, and William Bates, Thomas Jacombe (1622/3-87) and John Collinges (1623/4-99), who did not.

At the bishops' request the Presbyterians presented a number of exceptions and later a new liturgy hurriedly drawn up by Baxter. The Presbyterians were concerned that whatever liturgy was adopted there should be latitude for those whose consciences scrupled at certain points. The bishops objected to the Presbyterian exceptions, which argued for the words 'minister' instead of 'priest' and 'curate', and 'Lord's Day' instead of 'Sunday'; for fewer Apocryphal readings; against assuming all who they buried were Christians, and several other matters.

When time was almost gone, a hasty attempt was made to simplify the debate. Three disputants were chosen from each side, including divinity professor Peter Gunning (1614-84) on one side and Baxter on the other, according to Gilbert Burnet (1643-1715), the two 'most unfit to heal matters, and the fittest to widen them'. It was agreed that the Presbyterians should distinguish between what they thought sinful and what they opposed only as inexpedient, with attention being given to the former. The Presbyterians specified eight items. These were, according to Daniel Neal, the insistence that

1. No minister be admitted to baptise without using the sign of the cross.

2. No minister be admitted to officiate without wearing a surplice.

3. None be admitted to the Lord's Supper without kneeling.

4. Ministers are obliged to pronounce all baptised persons regenerated by the Holy Ghost, whether children of Christians or not.

5. Ministers are obliged to deliver the sacrament of the body and blood of Christ to the unfit both in health and sickness, and that by personal application, putting it into their hands, even those who are forced to receive it against their wills, through consciousness of their impenitency.

6. Ministers are obliged to absolve the unfit, and that in absolute expressions.

7. Ministers are forced to give thanks for all whom they bury, as brethren whom God has taken to himself.

8. None may be preachers who do not subscribe that there is nothing in the Common Prayer-book, book of ordination, and the Thirty-Nine Articles, contrary to the Word of God.

The bishops maintained that commanding an act which in itself lawful cannot be sinful. Baxter replied that the sin was not in commanding a lawful act but in forbidding the omission of an act that, though lawful, was also indifferent.

The conference broke up on 25 July, according to Burnet, 'without doing any good'. Bayne calls it 'a farce'. Burnet says:

It did rather hurt, and heightened the sharpness that was then on people's minds to such a degree that it needed no addition to raise it higher. The Presbyterians laid their complaints before the King but little regard was had to them; and now all the concern that seemed to employ the Bishops' thoughts was, not only to make no alteration on their own account, but to make the terms of conformity much stricter than ... before the war.

At the close of the conference, Baxter drafted the final report, where he wrote of waiting in hope

... that so great a calamity of your people, as would follow the loss of so many able faithful ministers as rigorous impositions would cast out, shall never be recorded in the history of your reign.

That hope was not to be.

Cragg says that before the conference terminated 'it was apparent that the important decisions would be made elsewhere'. Already the Church of England's two Houses of Convocation had assembled. The ruling party, having resolved to disregard the conscientious scruples of their opponents, proceeded to take measures for the full enforcement of their own ecclesiastical system. They were content, in Baxter's words, to sell their innocency 'and the Church's peace for nothing'.

The revised Prayer Book they produced — now making extensive use of the Authorized Version — contained a number of changes. There were a few new collects such as the prayer for all conditions of men and the general thanksgiving and one for Parliament, in which Charles is referred to as 'our most religious king'. 'A signification that was no way applicable to the king,' says Burnet. There was also a form for baptizing older persons. Kneeling at the sacrament was restored but with a word against the Roman idea of the real presence. Other changes included new holy days, such as St Barnabas and the conversion of St Paul and more lessons from the Apocrypha, in particular from the story of Bel and the Dragon. New offices were also drawn up for two new days, 30 January, called King Charles the Martyr, and 29 May, to mark King Charles II's restoration. There were some six hundred changes to the 1559 book altogether, mostly minor, giving the Puritans little of what they wanted and in some cases taking the book in a Romeward direction. Baxter complained that the new book was 'more grievous than before'.

## The new Parliament

In December 1660 the Convention Parliament was prorogued and in May 1661, the new Cavalier Parliament sat for the first time. Bayne calls it 'blindly, foolishly, furiously loyal'. It 'rushed at once with headlong impetuosity on Puritanism and the Puritans'. They instructed the hangman to publicly burn the Solemn League and Covenant, the agreement of 1643 between the Scots Covenanters and the English Parliament to introduce Scots Presbyterianism in England. At the same time episcopalianism was fully restored and the bishops were recalled to the House of Lords.

Aware that the Quakers refused all oaths, they also passed the Quaker Act, making it illegal not to swear allegiance to the king or for more than five Quakers to meet together on pain of fines, imprisonment or transportation for a third offence.

One gets an idea of how matters were unfolding from the entries highlighted by Stanford in Philip Henry's diary (16 June, 7 July, 25 July, 8 September, and 19 October 1661):

> Strong reports I should not be suffered to preach today; but I did; and no disturbance. Blessed be God, who hath my enemies in a chain!

> In despite of my enemies, the Lord hath granted the liberty of one Sabbath more. To Him be praise.

> Common Prayer-book tendered again. Lord, they devise wicked devices against me; but in thee do I put my trust. Father, forgive them!

> They took the cushion from me, but the pulpit was left. Blessed be God!

> Day of preparation for the sacrament... The good Lord pardon! Full of fears lest we should be hindered; for our adversaries bite the lip at us.

By this stage prospects for Presbyterians and the other Puritans did not look good. If Puritanism was not about to be destroyed quite, as Watts puts it, certainly 'the Puritan dream of reforming the Church of England from within', as he also suggests, was about to come to an end. In the words of Lloyd-Jones, 'the hope of the Puritans was finally dashed to the ground. It was their final defeat, and the exploding of all their longings.'

# 4 | 'WE WOULD HAVE MADE IT STRAITER' — THE GREAT EJECTION

**A**s we have seen, as early as September 1660 the king had given his consent to 'An act for confirming and restoring ministers', compelling nearly seven hundred parish ministers to vacate their livings. Many more were to follow.

## Bedford

As soon as Charles was declared king, the Bedfordshire magistrates ordered the restoration of the Prayer Book in public worship. Bunyan inevitably fell foul of the law and was famously imprisoned for the next twelve years. No doubt it was in this period that he began his famous *Pilgrim's Progress*. He was only one of many Puritans who, in God's providence, used their enforced silence to write.

Between 1661 and 1665 four further acts were passed against the Puritans, acts that since the nineteenth century have together been known as the Clarendon Code. They are named for the first Lord Clarendon, Edward Hyde (1609-74), who was Charles's Lord Chancellor until his exile in 1667. Though associated with the acts, Clarendon was not their author, and historians are divided on the question of the extent to which he approved of the code.

## The Corporation Act

The first of the four acts was the Corporation Act passed in December 1661. This act required three things from all municipal officials — mayors, aldermen, councillors, borough officials. These were an oath of allegiance to the throne, a formal rejection of the Solemn League and Covenant and the taking of communion in the parish church within a year of taking office.

The effect of the act was to exclude Nonconformists from public office and some conscientious Dissenters lost important posts as a result. Further, some unscrupulous corporations took advantage of the situation and voted such men into office then fined them when they declined to serve! Watts names eight cities, including Coventry and London, where this happened.

## The Act of Uniformity

Obviously, with the ascent of a new ruler, a new Act of Conformity was expected. Once Charles's new Parliament was in place they brought in such a bill. The bill that they passed was so strict that it was almost impossible for even the least dogmatic of the Puritans to accept it with a clear conscience.

Under British law, bills are presented to the House of Commons and the House of Lords and go through three readings in each house before receiving royal assent. The Act of Uniformity was given a first reading in the Commons on 29 June 1661 and was brought to the Lords on 10 July, not receiving its final reading there until 9 April 1662. After some to-ing and fro-ing between the Commons and Lords the bill was ready by 19 May 1662. Charles gave it his royal assent on 29 July 1662. It gave all ministers of the Church of England, university fellows, school teachers and private tutors too, until 24 August, St Bartholomew's Day, to conform to its demands or be ejected.

Among these demands were that ministers affirm the supremacy of the monarch in all things ecclesiastical and spiritual and to signify that they gave 'unfeigned assent' to everything in the forth-coming Book of Common Prayer. Most were unable to see this book in time, as it was not published until 6 August, though some came up to London for that express purpose. The philosopher John Locke (1632-1704) noted this, saying:

> And it is upon this occasion worth your knowledge, that so great was the zeal in carrying on this church affair, and so blind was the obedience required, that if you compute the time of the passing this act, with the time allowed for the clergy to subscribe the book of Common-Prayer thereby established; you shall plainly find it could not be printed and distributed so as one man in forty could have seen and read the book they did so perfectly assent and consent to.

Those who had not been ordained by a bishop were also expected to be re-ordained.

Further, there was again the need to repudiate the hated Solemn League and Covenant and to acknowledge that the oath taken to maintain it involved no moral obligation. A declaration was also required that it was unlawful under any pretence whatever to take up arms against the king.

The choice of St Bartholomew's Day over St Michael's Day, 29 September, for the implementation of the act was deliberate and cruel. A motion to put the date back to Michaelmas, when a minister's tithes were due, was lost by nine votes. Another for allowing ejected ministers one-fifth of the income from their livings, as had happened with those sequestered under Cromwell, was lost by seven votes.

By staying with the Bartholomean date, therefore, the government ensured that any who did not conform were deprived of a whole year's income. This is quite different to the arrangements when men were ejected in Cromwell's day. Quite apart from that, for any good Protestant the infamous massacre in France of St Bartholomew's Day 1572, was now inextricably linked with this new date.

Writing on the Cavalier Parliament, Paul Seaward comments that the combined effect of this act and previous ones 'created a measure far in excess of the government's intentions, which rather than coaxing presbyterians back to the Church' (as intended) 'would expel many even of the most moderate'.

## The Great Ejection

Estimates vary but it seems that, including those ejected before 1662 and some who jumped rather than waiting to be pushed, nearly two thousand ministers and others were silenced or ejected. There will always be some vagueness about the figure as some changed their minds. A. G. Matthews says that some 210 later conformed. A contemporary writer, John Walker, says of an Evan Griffiths of Oxwich in South Wales, who was ejected but then conformed, became as violent against Dissenters as he had once been against Royalists. Also, the ejection included not only ministers but also lecturers and even private tutors. Further, some such as Cornishman Francis Howell (1625-79) present anomalies. Howell, 'a man mighty in the scriptures' according to Calamy, was expelled both as Principal of Jesus College, Oxford, in 1660 and then as incumbent of Llanrhaeadr-ym-Mochnant in North Wales.

In his *Nonconformist Memorial* Calamy deals with some 2,465 people altogether. Matthews and Watts say that the number unwilling to conform in 1662 was 2,029, most in England and 120 in Wales. Some 200 of these were university lecturers. Matthews points out that a further 129 were deprived at an uncertain date between 1660 and 1663 and with the ejections of 1660 as well, he gives a total of 1,760 ministers (which is about 20% of the clergy) thrust out of the Church of England, silenced from preaching or teaching by law and so deprived of a livelihood.

Gerald Bray comments that 'almost all of these were Puritans, and so the Act may be said to represent the expulsion of Puritanism from the national Church'. On the other hand, John Spurr points out that Puritans remained within the state church and others, like Quakers and General Baptists, were ejected. He quotes John Corbet (1620-80), saying:

> ... it is a palpable injury to burden us with the various parties with whom we are now herded by our ejection in the general state of dissenters.

Ejected from Bramshot, Hertfordshire, Corbet was, according to Baxter 'of extraordinary judgment, stayedness, moderation, peaceable principles and blameless life, a solid preacher, well known by his writings'. 'A great man every way', wrote Calamy.

Most of those ejected were Presbyterian, though some 194 were Independent (154 in parishes, twenty-four in Wales; twenty-eight lecturers or chaplains and twelve academics). There were also nineteen Baptists (eleven in Wales). Historian Daniel Neal tells us that when the Earl of Manchester told the king that he was afraid that the terms of the act were so harsh many ministers would not comply, Bishop Sheldon replied that he was rather afraid they would. However, he added, as they had declared themselves so openly, 'we will make them all knaves' if they do. Also when Dr Allen, the clerk of the 1661 convocation, said that it was a pity that 'the door is so strait' Sheldon answered, '... it is no pity at all; if we had thought so many of them would have conformed, we would have made it straiter'. On the other hand, a man like Bishop Robert Sanderson (1587-1663), who had been ejected by Cromwell's men in 1648, was much milder, conceding that more was imposed on ministers than he wished had been.

As pointed out earlier, the Dissenters objected to many important details in the Prayer Book. Importantly, they refused 'to pronounce all baptised persons regenerated by the Holy Ghost' and regarded it as sinful to give the communion elements to the unfit, to pronounce a general absolution or to declare everyone they buried 'our dear brother here departed'.

They also objected to the stipulation that any who had not been ordained by a bishop, as was the case with many in Cromwell's time, had to be re-ordained. When asked to give one reason for his Nonconformity by his old friend Seth Ward (1617-89) — then Bishop of Exeter — John Howe (1630-1705) instanced re-ordination. 'Pray, Sir,' said the bishop, 'what hurt is there in being twice ordained?' 'Hurt, my lord,' Howe famously answered:

> ... it hurts my understanding; the thought is shocking; it is an absurdity, since nothing can have two beginnings. I am sure I am a minister of Christ, and am ready to debate that matter with you, if your lordship pleases, but I cannot begin again to be a minister.

Robert Adkins (1626-85), who Calamy describes as having 'a large heart and an open hand', was ejected first from Exeter Cathedral in 1660, complaining of 'church music jostling out the constant preaching of the word', then from St John's, Exeter, in 1662, when he spoke for many in his farewell sermon, saying:

> Let him never be accounted a sound christian that doth not fear God and honour the king. I beg that you would not suffer our nonconformity, for which we patiently bear the loss of our places, to be an act of unpeaceableness and disloyalty. We will do anything for his majesty but sin. We will hazard anything for him but our souls. We hope we could die for him, only we dare not be damned for him. We make no question, however we may be

accounted of here, we shall be found loyal and obedient subjects at our appearance before God's tribunal.

## No Sunday like it

As the date approached there was some nervousness on the part of the government as to whether there would be any kind of insurrection. New regiments were raised and other measures were taken to be on the safe side. In the end, the ejection took place with the minimum of commotion.

On 10 August the diarist Samuel Pepys wrote, 'the new service-book (which is now lately come forth)' — i.e. the Book of Common Prayer —

> … was laid upon their desk at St Sepulchre's for Mr Gouge to read; but he laid it aside, and would not meddle with it: and I perceive the Presbyters do all prepare to give over all against Bartholomew-tide. Mr Herring, being lately turned out at St Bride's, did read the psalm to the people while they sung at Dr Bates's, which methought is a strange turn… So home with Mrs Turner, and there hear that Mr Calamy hath taken his farewell this day of his people, and that others will do so the next Sunday.

The references are to Thomas Gouge (1605-81), son of William Gouge (1575-1653), who was based in London but worked extensively in Wales and was the author of several practical works (he was one of the most moderate of Nonconformists and would have taken the oath demanded by the Five Mile Act if Manton had not dissuaded him); to John Herring (d. *c.* 1672); to William Bates and to Edmund Calamy the elder.

Most ejected men took opportunity to preach farewell sermons where they could, usually on the Sunday before the ejectment took place, 17 August. Some preached more than one sermon. Iain Murray quotes Stoughton's description:

No Sunday in England ever resembled exactly that which fell on the 17th of August, 1662, one week before the feast of St Bartholomew. There have been 'mourning, lamentation, and woe,' in particular parish churches when death, persecution, or some other cause has broken pastoral ties, and severed from loving congregations their spiritual guides; but for many hundreds of ministers on the same day to be uttering farewells is an unparalleled circumstance. In after years, Puritan fathers and mothers related to their children the story of assembled crowds, of aisles, standing-places and stairs, filled to suffocation, of people clinging to open windows like swarms of bees, of overflowing throngs in churchyards and streets, of deep silence or stifled sobs, as the flock gazed on the shepherd — 'sorrowing most of all that they should see his face no more.'

Murray himself says:

The atmosphere of that day was electric and charged with emotion; the popular discontent was great and strong guards stood ready in London, but these sermons seem far removed from all that. There is a calmness, and unction and a lack of invective. Great though their sorrow was for their flocks and for their nation, they had a message to preach which was more than equal to the strain of the crisis. An eternal God, an Ever-Living Saviour and a glorious hope of heaven, carried them through this heaviest trial.

Pepys wrote on 17 August:

Up very early, this being the last Sunday that the Presbyterians are to preach, unless they read the new Common Prayer and renounce the Covenant, and so I had a mind to hear Dr Bates's farewell sermon, and walked thither, calling first at my brother's ... and so walked to St Dunstan's, where, it not being seven o'clock yet, the doors were not open... At eight o'clock I went, and crowded in at a back door among others, the church being half-full almost before any doors were open publicly; which is the first time that I have done so these many years since I used to go with my father and mother, and so got into the gallery, beside the pulpit, and heard very well. His text was, 'Now the God of Peace—' the last Hebrews, and the 20<sup>th</sup> verse: he making a very good sermon, and very little reflections in it to any thing of the times. Besides the sermon, I was very well pleased with the sight of a fine lady...

So to Madam Turner's, and dined with her. She had heard Parson Herring take his leave; though he, by reading so much of the Common Prayer as he did, hath cast himself out of the good opinion of both sides.

After dinner to St Dunstan's again; and the church quite crowded before I came, which was just at one o'clock; but I got into the gallery again, but stood in a crowd and did exceedingly sweat all the time. He pursued his text again very well; and only at the conclusion told us, after this manner: 'I do believe that many of you do expect that I should say something to you in reference to the time, this being the last time that possibly I may appear here. You know it is not my manner to speak any thing in the pulpit that is extraneous to my text and business; yet this I shall say, that it is not my opinion, fashion, or humour that keeps me from complying with what is required of us; but something which, after much prayer, discourse, and study yet remains unsatisfied, and commands me herein. Wherefore, if it is my unhappiness not to receive such an illumination as should direct me to do otherwise, I know no reason why men should not pardon me in this world, and am confident that God will pardon me for it in the next.' And so he concluded.

Parson Herring read a psalm and chapters before sermon; and one was the chapter in the Acts, where the story of Ananias and Sapphira is. And after he had done, says he, 'This is just the case of England at present. God he bids us to preach, and men bid us not to preach; and if we do, we are to be imprisoned and further punished. All that I can say to it is, that I beg your prayers, and the prayers of all good Christians, for us.' This was all the exposition he made of the chapter in these very words, and no more.

... I hear most of the Presbyters took their leaves today, and that the City is much dissatisfied with it. I pray God keep peace among us, and make the Bishops careful of bringing in goodmen in their rooms, or else all will fly a-pieces; for bad ones will not [go] down with the City.

## The First Conventicle Act

To back up the Act of Uniformity, Parliament later introduced penal acts intended to destroy the many independent groups, Congregational or Baptist, that continued to meet.

In February 1663 Charles made a vain attempt to have the Corporation Act and the Act of Uniformity repealed but Parliament resisted. As if to vindicate Parliament's caution, news came the following month of a conspiracy known as the Derwentdale Plot that apparently involved plans to murder members of the clergy. Frustrated Dissenters in County Durham had succumbed to the temptation to take the law into their own hands. In August came the arrest of the ringleaders of a gang planning to seize York Castle with similar aims. In October Farnley Wood near Leeds was the centre for what was supposed to be a nationwide rising. More than twenty men were arrested and in January 1664 hanged, drawn and quartered as traitors.

By May 1664 Parliament had every excuse it could want, therefore, to pass the First Conventicle Act. The act banned conventicles, that is, religious assemblies of more than five people over the age of sixteen apart from family members, unless they used Church of England rites. The penalties for breaking this law were made very strict. A first offence merited three months in prison or a £5 fine. A second offence saw the penalty doubled and a third would meet with transportation to America for seven years or a fine of £100.

## The Five Mile Act

The next year, in October 1665, the Act for Restraining Non-Conformists from Inhabiting in Corporations or the Five Mile Act was passed. Watts calls this further act indefensible. It appears to have been specifically and spitefully aimed at certain godly ministers.

When the Great Plague afflicted London in 1665, a plague that was preceded by a terrible drought, it killed some 70,000 of the population of only half a million. Parliament moved to Oxford and most, though not all, Anglican ministers fled to the countryside. Seeing the need, many of the ejected ministers earned great credit by going into the city and looking after people. The best known of these was Thomas Vincent (1634-78), who Beth Lynch describes as 'a formidably eloquent and learned man, who reputedly knew the entire New Testament and Psalms by heart ... at once selfless and single-minded in his ministry ... he does indeed seem, as Slater states [in his funeral sermon], to have been "freely willing to venture his life for the salvation of souls".' Vincent wrote about the plague and the fire of the following year in his book *God's Terrible Voice in the City.*

Others who acted in a similar way included the silenced James Janeway (1636-74), who Baxter calls 'a humble, a serious, a peaceable, and an industrious spirit: his heart ... set on the work of God, and the winning of souls'. He was an author who wrote much of Christian experience, producing books on children's conversions and providences at sea among other works. There were also Robert Franklin (1630-1703), who originally ministered in Suffolk but, for the sake of conscience, moved to London, where he later spent some time in prison for his Nonconformity; John Turner (c. 1629-92) and Robert Chambers from Ireland, who went under the alias of John Grimes. Samuel Annesley (1620-96) was another, the editor of the sermon series *The Morning-Exercise at Cripple-Gate* and the father of Susanna Wesley.

The Five Mile Act specifically forbade ministers to go within five miles of any city, corporation or borough, or any parish where they had been minister or conducted unlawful conventicles. It also required a new oath, 'the Oxford oath', by which a minister would swear never to attempt any change of government in church or state. Neal comments that 'it will amaze all posterity, that in a time both of war and pestilence' (beside the plague, England was again at war with the Netherlands, 1665-67),

> ... and when the Nonconformist ministers were hazarding their lives in the service of the souls of the distressed and dying citizens of London, that the prime-minister and his creatures, instead of mourning for the nation's sins, and meditating are formation of manners, should pour out all their vengeance upon the Nonconformists, in order to make their condition more insupportable. One would have thought such a judgement from Heaven, and such a generous compassion in the ejected ministers, should have softened the hearts of their most cruel enemies; but the Presbyterians must be crushed, in defiance of the rebukes of Providence.

The punishment for this 'crime' was a £40 fine, a third going to the king, a third to the poor and a third to the complainant. The only way out of it was by giving the objectionable oath mentioned. If a man refused that oath he would be banned not just from preaching but from any form of teaching or tutoring too, the most obvious way for such a person to make a living.

It is this act that now drove ministers into obscure and isolated places and that necessitated long, secret journeys in order to circumvent the law. This is when secret meetings began to take place and when tricks such as having the minister preach in one room while the congregation listened in another began to come in.

The act expired on 1 March 1669 and with the fall of Clarendon in 1667 there was some relief for the Dissenters. This was short-lived, however, as in July 1669, prompted by Parliament, the king made a proclamation urging magistrates to continue to use the outstanding laws against Nonconformists.

## The Second Conventicle Act

A new conventicle bill was not possible straight away because Charles had prorogued Parliament in November 1669. By

February 1670, however, a lack of money forced him to recall Parliament and soon a Second Conventicle Act had been passed. It was famously described by Andrew Marvell as 'the quintessence of arbitrary malice'. Penalties for ordinary worshippers were reduced to five shillings and ten shillings for a second offence but fines for preachers and the owners of places where conventicles were found went up to £20 for a first offence and £40 for a second one. The idea of distraint was also introduced, the seizure of a person's property in order to obtain payment. If the minister could not pay, wealthier members of the congregation could lawfully be plundered. Magistrates who refused to implement the act would themselves be fined £100.

## Religious apartheid

In 1672 Charles issued a Declaration of Indulgence, which allowed Nonconformists to apply for licences to preach and to establish meeting places where they could meet openly. The following year that was repealed and the first Test Act was brought in. This required all in public office to take communion in the Church of England. In this way Nonconformists were debarred from public office (and a university education) unless they were prepared to compromise their consciences.

In other ways the 1670s were a time of relative quiet for Nonconformists. However, in 1681 a new wave of persecution began against them and it was not until 1689 that the whole period of suffering would finally end with the Act of Toleration.

Contrasting the Cromwellian Protectorate favourably with the subsequent period, the historian Barry Coward has written provocatively of the narrowness and ferociousness of the Clarendon Code and the 'system of religious apartheid' it created, reserving 'political office and a university education only for card carrying members of the Church of England' and condemning Dissenters to 'the status of second-class citizens, liable (at best) to exclusion from political life and (at worst) to suffer imprisonment or transportation'. The analogy may be overdrawn but perhaps by it those who know something of what happened in South Africa in the twentieth century may begin to grasp something of the way life was in England from 1660 to 1689.

# 5 | 'LIKE LAMBS, WITHOUT ANY RESISTANCE' — THE GREAT PERSECUTION

In August 1664 the diarist Samuel Pepys wrote:

> While we were talking came by several poor creatures carried by, by constables, for being at a conventicle. They go like lambs, without any resistance. I would to God they would either conform, or be more wise, and not be catched!

Right from the beginning of Charles's reign there was persecution against faithful Christians. As the years went by matters generally deteriorated, especially from 1681, for the increasingly indistinguishable Separatists and Dissenters, although it is true that there were periods of relief. The Broadmead Baptists wrote of some eight waves of persecution and it is clear that, as is often the case to this day, persecution did come in waves. Typically again, it varied in form and intensity, from minor harassment to mass imprisonment, and there were various factors involved.

## Blatancy

Firstly, to some extent it depended on one's attitude to the law and to compromise. The Quakers bore the brunt of the persecution as they usually were not prepared to accept any compromise whatsoever. Certainly at first, most of them felt it wrong to hide away from the authorities and so even when their buildings were demolished they would assemble amid the rubble. Others took the same attitude. A Baptist congregation in Kent disciplined a member who they accused of making their knees feeble and their heads hang down by his advocacy of hiding lights under bushels by 'creeping into corners, and meeting by fours'. Others, with good conscience, took appropriate steps to conceal their activities. An Independent church in Norwich met 'in small parcels'.

## Variety

Michael Watts suggests that the Presbyterians were the most diverse in approach. At one extreme were some who simply stopped exercising a public ministry and attended the parish church. Watts mentions Richard Bell (1615-86), previously vicar of Polesworth, who Calamy says was a faithful man,

> But after this last ejectment, he had no place left him to preach at, with satisfaction to his conscience. And therefore his mouth being stopped here, he quietly set up his staff, and spent his time in profitable conversation with Mr Samuel Hildersham.

This happened in the Erdington area near Birmingham. A Westminster Divine, Samuel Hildersham (1594?-1674), who was also ejected in 1662, was the son of the Puritan Arthur Hildersham (1563-1632). Watts also mentions Jerome Littlejohn (1625-80), who, Matthews says, lived 'very privately never attempting anything against the peace and quiet either of church or state'. Also Irish-born Zachary Crofton (1626-72), 'the best known Presbyterian controversialist in the Restoration' was imprisoned for tirades against the bishops but when confined to the Tower in 1661 went to common prayer. A father of seven, he worked as a farmer, a grocer and a teacher after the ejection. As we have stated, some 210 Dissenters later conformed and another fifty were prepared to take the non-resistance oath prescribed by the Five Mile Act. These included the godly author Thomas Watson (d. 1686).

At the other extreme were those who, once ejected, refused to have anything further to do with the established church. Watts mentions John Cole (*c.* 1621-73) from East Anglia, arrested while preaching in his house and imprisoned from 1664 to 1672 and Robert Collins in Devon, mentioned in Chapter 1, who was often fined and imprisoned. Matthews says that at least thirty-five Presbyterian ministers were excommunicated after the ejection, usually for non-attendance.

Most perhaps were somewhere in the middle. While living in Acton in the period between the two conventicle acts Baxter preached at home to all who came, but once he had finished he headed, with his congregation, to the parish church. Northerner Oliver Heywood (1630-1702) pursued a similar policy, even preaching in his old pulpit when his successor was away, as did John French (d. 1691) of Wenvoe near Cardiff, who would attend the parish church then preach in his own house afterwards.

To keep within the law, another northerner, Adam Martindale (1623-86), used his mathematical skills to divide his auditors into small groups to whom he preached the same sermon several times in a day. In Derbyshire, John Hieron (1606-82) 'preached twice a day in the biggest families with four persons only besides; but as many under sixteen years of age as would come'. Obadiah Grew (1607-89) dictated a new sermon to a secretary every week and

> ... sent it to be read, to four or more writers in shorthand every
> Saturday night or Lord's Day morning; and every one of these

read it to four new men who transcribed it also: and so it was afterwards read at twenty several meetings.

Vincent Alsop (1630-1703), ejected from Wilby in Northamptonshire in 1662, divided his Tothill Street, Westminster, congregation in two. Each half met separately in a private home once a fortnight to take the sacrament.

Like other persecuted peoples since, they sometimes disguised their meetings as feasts. If they were disturbed, they would put their Bibles away and pretend to be making merry. Some would meet at unusual times, sometimes in the small hours of night. The Congregational Church in Stepney had a concealed room in the ceiling of their meeting place. Dissenters in Olney would meet at the point where Buckinghamshire, Bedfordshire and Northamptonshire converge so as to be able to escape from one to the other quickly should the authorities arrive from one or other of the counties! In Devon the famous John Flavel (1630-91) would preach on the Saltstone, a ledge in the middle of the Salcombe estuary accessible only at low water during spring tides. On one occasion he rode to Totnes disguised as a woman in order to carry out a baptism. Another time, pursued by riders, he plunged his horse into the sea and escaped arrest by swimming round the rocks to Slapton Sands. Watts also mentions Stephen Hughes (1622-88) and Rhys Prydderch (*c.* 1620-99), who preached in caves in Carmarthenshire.

The Broadmead Baptists in Bristol describe at length how they were constantly harassed by the mayor. They would put youths at the door as look-outs and eluded his violent attempts to break in by escaping through cellars and cupboards that led into hidden rooms. After having several pastors imprisoned they came up with the idea of hanging a curtain in their meeting place behind which the minister could stand to preach, preventing any informers seeing what he looked like. Even more ingeniously,

> Brother Gifford's people took this course: a company of tall brethren stand about him that speaks, and having near his feet

made a trap-door in the floor, when the informers come they let down the brother that spake into a room below.

Another ruse, in consultation with the Presbyterians, Congregationalists and other Baptists, was to hold meetings every night of the week and so weary the authorities who eventually decided they could give only one night a week to investigating such crimes.

In 1665 Broadmead excommunicated six members 'some for neglecting their duty of assembling through fear'. Such fear is understandable when we consider the malice and violence with which the law was enforced in many cases.

## Protecting ministers

Great efforts were made to protect ministers. Richard Chantry (d. 1694) would dress as an agricultural labourer and walk to worship in the twilight 'with a Bible in his pocket and a fork on his shoulder'. When constables arrived to arrest Thomas Vincent the congregation sang a psalm and he was able to make good his escape. On another occasion, in Brighton, the Scot William Wallace (d. 1678) was saved when several pregnant women put themselves in the way of the advancing officers.

Joseph Oddy (1629-87) in Cambridgeshire would often preach in a wood at night mounted on a horse, ready to escape if needs be. Oliver Heywood's friend Thomas Jollie (1629-1703) would preach on the stairs behind a stable door where the bottom half remained closed and the top half could be closed if and when necessary.

## Fines and distraint

When Dissenters were caught preaching they were fined or imprisoned; some even died. Fines were often ruinous and were intended to be so. In Cornwall Thomas Tregosse (d. c. 1671) had paid £220 in fines by the time of his death. After being fined several times Robert Collins sold his house and estate and fled to the Netherlands.

Because the Second Conventicle Act allowed distraint, working men were sometimes deprived of the very tools they used to make a living. Watts instances the case of poor heelmaker Thomas Cooper of Bedford, who had three loads of wood taken and in another case £500 worth of livestock and produce were seized to cover a £220 fine. This contrasts with those who were making easy money, informers such as an innkeeper in Richmond, Yorkshire, who collected £2,000 in fourteen months.

In Flintham, Nottingham, the fury was so great that John James (*fl.* 1669-78) not only lost £500 in goods but one of his children died of fright. In 1664 in Winslow in Buckinghamshire Benjamin Keach (1640-1704), still then a General Baptist, was pilloried and had the valuable stock of a children's book he had written taken and destroyed. In 1680 Bunyan's main publisher, Francis Smith (d. 1691), claimed to have lost more than £1,400 in twenty years by having books seized and then sold for profit.

## Prison and death

Prisons varied greatly in Restoration England. The instructions of magistrates and the kindness or otherwise of prison-keepers made a big difference. None were four-star hotels but some prisoners had reasonable comfort. Often prisoners were allowed out not only to see family but even, ironically, to preach at conventicles, as long as they returned at night. Calamy says John Farroll (*c.* 1623-1703), arrested for preaching in Godalming in 1669 and kept in Marshalsea, Southwark, for six months, sometimes called it

> ... one of the most comfortable parts of his life, through the kindness of friends whom God raised up to administer relief to him in his troubles. His enemies said, that they would not send him to prison again, because he lived better there than at home.

It is well known that Bunyan was allowed out of prison at times and was even made pastor while in prison in January 1672. Thomas Rees says that William Jones (d. *c.* 1700) of Carmarthenshire was imprisoned in Haverfordwest but

> Having previously engaged to preach in a distant locality, he felt a strong desire to fulfil his engagement. An influential gentleman giving his word for his speedy return to the prison, the keeper permitted him to go. The gentleman lent him his horse and top coat.

The large crowd was 'filled with a strange mixture of joy and sadness' when he told them his story. After preaching, he returned to the prison. Vavasor Powell (1617-70) often preached in the Fleet prison and even preached outside on at least one occasion in 1669. When Baxter was briefly imprisoned in 1670 he speaks of it being

> ... no great suffering to me, for I had an honest gaoler, who showed me all the kindness he could. I had a large room, and the liberty of walking in a fair garden. My wife was never so cheerful a companion to me as in prison, and was very much against my seeking to be released. She had brought so many necessaries, that we kept house as contentedly and comfortably as at home, though in a narrow room, and I had the sight of more of my friends in a day, than I had at home in half a year.

It was in the heat of summer, though, and he wonders if perhaps they hoped he would die there!

Watts points out, on the other side, that 'many prisons were stinking holes and their keepers brutes'.

> The filthy, congested, foul-smelling Restoration gaols, unheated in winter and sweltering in summer, the breeding-ground of fever, plague and smallpox, took a fearful toll of Quaker lives.

And not just Quakers either. A. G. Matthews suggests that 12.4% of the ejected men who did not conform — some 215 altogether — were imprisoned between 1662 and the death of Charles II in 1685. Most imprisonments were for short periods but others were lengthy terms — the Congregationalist and 'Apostle of Cambridgeshire' Francis Holcroft (1628/9-92) spent nine years in prison (apart from a few months in 1672 he was hardly out of prison from 1672 to 1680); Congregationalist Richard Worts (d. 1686), seven years; Presbyterian Cole, eight years. For part of the time, Cole was in Norwich Castle, with six others, says Calamy,

> ... in a hole in the wall, which had neither door, window, nor chimney; and room but for one truckle-bed; the rest lay in hammocks. The hole had three wickets into the felons yard, one of which was of necessity open night and day or they must have been stifled with the steam of the charcoal.

At least seven of the ejected clergy died in prison. These included Vavasor Powell, who died in 1670, having been imprisoned in 1659; John Thompson of Bristol, who died in March 1675; Francis Bampfield, who died in Newgate in 1684 after years of imprisonment, as did the London Presbyterian William Jenkyn (1613-85) and Thomas Delaune (1635-85) and his family.

Jenkyn's daughter gave out mourning rings at the funeral engraved with the words 'William Jenkyn, murdered in Newgate'. It was said that a nobleman, having heard of Jenkyn's death, said to the king, 'May it please your Majesty, Jenkyn has got his liberty'. In reply he eagerly asked who had given it to him. The nobleman replied, 'A greater than your Majesty, the King of kings'. Charles, who was not long for this world himself, appeared struck and remained silent.

The Broadmead records reveal that on one occasion their notorious persecutor John Hellier, on discovering a Dissenting meeting, had his men chase

> ... Mr Knight, a minister of Taunton, and Mr Ford, a Bristol mercer, for half a mile, vociferating, 'Knock 'em down,' so that

onlookers thought they were hunting deer. Ford and Knight, not thinking the water deep, sought to re-cross the river by wading, when the former began to sink and cried out for help.

Their pursuers, 'instead of succouring them, ran off, when a Kingswood collier plunged in and with great difficulty saved Mr Knight, but Ford was drowned'. Knight also died subsequently. The Baptist pastor George Fownes died in prison in Gloucester in November 1685.

Others emerged from their ordeal with permanent damage to their health.

> John Cromwell [d. 1685], imprisoned for three years in Newark gaol, emerged suffering from asthma, scurvy, and dropsy; John Hoppin [d. 1705], after six months in 'a very cold chamber' in the Southgate prison, Exeter, 'thereby got such a rheumatism as rendered him a perfect cripple to the day of his death'.

The former Cromwellian Trier, the Baptist Henry Jessey (1601-63), who had also been imprisoned in the time of Charles I, found himself under arrest again in 1661 and died aged sixty in September 1663, six months after release.


## Providence

There was a Bible-taught confidence among the Dissenters that their sufferings were working for them 'a far more exceeding and eternal weight of glory'. When Joseph Oddy, mentioned above, was taunted by a Cambridge wit with the doggerel lines:

> Good day, Mr. Oddy,
> Pray how fares your body;
> Methinks you look damnably thin?

He shot straight back with:

That sir's your mistake,
'Tis for righteousness' sake;
Damnation's the fruit of your sin.

The Dissenters were not slow to see in various providences the hand of God encouraging them and dealing with their persecutors. What else could one make of the Great Plague of 1665, the Great Fire of London of 1666 and the war with the Dutch too, for that matter? 'Nonconformist writings abound,' says Watts, 'in stories of disasters which befell individual persecutors.'

Positively, Philip Henry once observed in his old age that though many of the ejected ministers were brought very low, had many mouths to feed, and were greatly harassed by persecution, and though their friends were generally poor and unable to support them, yet, in all his acquaintance, he never knew nor could remember to have heard of any Nonconformist minister being in prison for debt.

Once when Oliver Heywood was in great need, he called his servant, Martha, who had refused to desert the family in their distress, and told her to take a basket, go to Halifax and call on a shopkeeper there and ask to borrow five shillings. If he was willing, she was to buy provisions there. Martha felt rather embarrassed and attempted several times to summon the courage to enter the shop and make the request. In a little while the shopkeeper saw her outside and thought he recognized her. He then told her that he had five guineas for her master from friends and had just started to wonder how he was going to get it to him. At that she burst into tears and told him what she had intended to say. He was moved by her story and told her to come to him whenever there was such a need.

Watts cites the example of a wealthy Lincolnshire man named Radley who attempted to harm a congregation of General Baptists only to become bankrupt and die of the plague, his widow and orphaned children being forced to cast themselves on the mercy of these very same Baptists. Philip Henry notes the death of magistrate David Morrice, a persecutor, thrown from his horse and drowned.

Thomas Robinson, MP for Helston, Cornwall, was gored by a bull and died on the very day he was intending to prosecute Dissenters.

On the second anniversary of Charles's coronation a mob in Wincanton, Somerset, held a mock trial of a Dissenting preacher and using an effigy of him with catechism in hand they dragged it on a hurdle through the town to the top of a hill, where they prepared a bonfire to burn the effigy hanging on a pole. The wind blew the fire out so they shot the effigy until it eventually fell into the flames and was consumed. It was observed by local people that a number of the ringleaders had one remarkable calamity or another befall them not long after. Some died very miserably. This was then written up in a published book of prodigies.

A typical and difficult-to-establish story would be that of soldiers coming to break up a meeting one Lord's Day in April 1682, and to take a Mr Browning of Rothwell, Northamptonshire. The constable admonished the soldiers to take care, as he had had previous experience of what could happen to those involved in persecution of Dissenters. A certain Justice – a great persecutor – once engaged eight soldiers of whom the constable had been one. The Justice had since died, as had six of the eight soldiers. Some were hanged and some broke their necks. The constable himself had fallen off his horse and broken his collarbone. 'It hath given me such warning,' he said, 'that, for my part, I am resolved I will never meddle with them any more.'

Watts also refers to the evangelist Henry Williams (1624-84) of Ysgafell, near Newtown in Mid-Wales. He spent nine years in prison, during which time his persecutors burnt down his house, abused his wife and apparently killed his aged father. At last they seized the very crops growing in the fields, determined to leave the family with nothing. There was, however, a field of recently sown wheat that they probably did not think worth destroying. That very field afterwards thrived and became the talk of the place and the wonder of the whole country all around. For two centuries the field was known as 'Cae'r fendith' (the field of blessing).

## Confidence

The Broadmead pastor Thomas Hardcastle (1637-78), Fownes' predecessor, sums up the prevailing attitude among the persecuted in a letter to his congregation at the time:

> It has been our great error that we have not trusted in the power of God. We have reasoned about the worst that men can do, but have not believed the best that God can do... We are sowing for posterity; the generation coming on will have the good fruit of this present persecution.

While not everyone remained true, generally speaking the Nonconformist cause continued to grow despite the persecution.

## Freedom

Although there was clearly a great deal of persecution of Dissenters it is important to recognize that in many instances either the local law-enforcers had no appetite for persecution, or public opinion would not stand for it. Informers were far from popular and often suffered themselves if they were discovered by an angry and hostile crowd. Juries were sometimes simply unwilling to convict a man no matter how demanding and harsh a judge may have been.

In the case of the Essex-based writer Giles Firmin (1613/14-97), he was apparently not molested by the authorities but enjoyed 'the favour and respect' of 'the neighbouring gentry and justices of peace' because like several others he had decided to practise medicine.

Not only that but the king himself on occasion stepped in to save the persecuted. In 1663 he was able to secure the release of Calamy from Newgate. Perhaps the best-known example is his intervention in 1664 on behalf of twelve Baptists in Aylesbury brought to his attention by Kiffin.

***

The way the penal laws were enforced against Dissenters was never as consistent as it might have been, and varied from place to place and from time to time. Nevertheless, the persecution was often fierce and it had a real and lasting impact not only for evil but in a remarkable way also for good.

# 6 | 'THE LIBERTIES OF ENGLAND' — WORKING TOWARDS THE ACT OF TOLERATION

**A**s we have suggested, the years 1662 to 1689 were not years of unremitting persecution. Even before the broad daylight of 1689 there were moments when the sun broke through and the persecution eased. John Spurr identifies the years 1663, 1667, 1668, 1673, 1674 and 1680 as the years before 1689 when Parliament was seriously debating comprehension and toleration. There were royal indulgences too, that of Charles in 1672 and that of James in 1683.

## The Indulgence of 1672

After the first ten years of persecution, there was a brief respite in 1672 when Charles published his Indulgence stating that as it was evident that the current policy was not working,

> ... we think ourself obliged to make use of that supreme power in ecclesiastical matters, which is not only inherent in us, but hath been declared and recognised to be so.

No doubt Charles had his Romanist friends in mind when he made this declaration but it would obviously have an effect on Nonconformists too.

The act was greeted with mixed feelings and some hesitation on the Dissenters' side. They were concerned firstly at the way that this liberty was being granted. (They would have been even more concerned if they had known that it was prompted in part by a promise by Charles to the French king Louis XIV to declare himself a Roman Catholic in return for financial reward.) The writer Daniel Defoe recalled the popular Presbyterian MP William Love, declaring himself to be a Dissenter and so 'unhappily obnoxious to the law' and one who would readily see the law against the Dissenters 'repealed by the same authority that made it' not meddled with by the king making a proclamation, even to his own hurt.

The royal proclamation made it possible, with the penal laws suspended, to have legally licensed ministers and meeting-houses. However, in order to register with the government the Dissenters would need to volunteer information about their ministers and meetings that could be used against them at some point in the future.

The more conservative Presbyterians could also see how the sanctioning of separate places of worship undermined parish order. The granting of toleration was likely to mean the demise of comprehension.

The Quakers refused to seek licences en masse and so did many Baptists and Congregationalists. However, a total of 1,610 ministers did take out licences. There were 939 Presbyterians, 458 Congregationalists or Independents, and 210 Baptists.

Some Dissenting meeting-houses had already been quietly built but now more were openly built and fitted out for public use. Thomas Watson, for example, had been able to build such a meeting-house following the Great Fire, in Bishopsgate, London. He was joined in his pastorate there by the illustrious Stephen Charnock (1628-80), formerly silenced by circumstances. Not far away was Samuel Annesley's meeting place. In Yorkshire Presbyterian Oliver Heywood formed a church on similar lines to those of the Independents. Presbyterian ordinations began again. Around five hundred Dissenters were pardoned, including Bunyan, his twelve-year stretch finally coming to an end.

The king's indulgence was not allowed to stand, however, because it was not an Act of Parliament. As soon as Charles needed money he had to recall Parliament and they soon overthrew the indulgence early in 1773. However, says Watts, 'the results of the twelve month's toleration could not be completely eradicated'. From then on, though the penal laws were sporadically renewed and there was further persecution, the scene had radically changed.

## The First Test Act

In 1673 the First Test Act was passed, 'An act for preventing dangers which may happen from popish recusants'. The act enforced on all persons filling any office — civil or military — the obligation of taking an oath of supremacy and allegiance and subscribing to a declaration against transubstantiation. They were also required to receive the sacrament in the national church within three months of admittance to office. The oath to be taken said:

> I, N, do declare that I do believe that there is not any transubstantiation in the sacrament of the Lord's Supper, or in the elements of the bread and wine, at or after the consecration thereof by any person whatsoever.

By requiring that communion be taken in the national church, the government effectively barred Nonconformists from public office (and a university education) unless they were prepared to compromise their consciences. Initially, this act did not include MPs but in 1678 another test act was passed, requiring that all peers and members of the House of Commons make a declaration against transubstantiation, invocation of saints and the sacrifice of the Mass. Though the primary effect of this act was to exclude Roman Catholics from both houses, it also hit Dissenters, as it meant that to hold office they had to practise 'occasional conformity', something that was odious to many.

The acts were also a blow to Charles's brother and heir to the throne, James the Duke of York, who was a secret Roman Catholic. He was forced to resign his position as Lord High Admiral, making his position completely clear. The king subsequently ordered James's two daughters to be brought up as Protestants, and they were married to Protestant men as a way of appeasing the country.

However, after the alleged 'Popish Plot' of 1678, where the infamous Titus Oates (1649-1705) made false accusations of popish intrigue leading to the executions of several innocent people, a wave of anti-Catholic sentiment ran through the country and James was *persona non grata* in England. Anthony Ashley Cooper (1621-83), Earl of Shaftesbury, who had been a member of Cromwell's Council of State and who was a very experienced politician, even began to agitate for James to be excluded from the line of succession. This led to a political stand-off as successive Parliaments threatened to pass such an Exclusion Bill but were dissolved. As these parliamentary battles went on, a good number of Dissenting MPs were elected, and were then able to throw their weight behind Shaftesbury, who returned the favour by pushing for comprehension and tolerance schemes to ease the burdens on Dissent.

## The 'Tory Revenge'

Then came a period known as the 'Tory Revenge'. Persecution up to this point had been sporadic but sometimes fierce. In 1681 the most severe persecution of the period began. 'We should be in no doubt,' writes Mark Goldie, 'about how explicitly persecution was demanded. Scarcely a tremor of embarrassment disturbed the voices of divines who called for "a holy violence", "a rigorous and seasonable execution of penal laws" against the "fanatic vermin" whose conventicles troubled the land.'

In London alone, according to John Coffey,

> ... over 3800 different people were arrested and brought before the courts between 1682 and 1686 for attending Nonconformist conventicles. London Dissent was terrorised by the Hilton gang, a band of over 40 thuggish informers who infiltrated meetings, gathered incriminating information, participated in prosecutions, and seized Dissenters' goods by force when they failed to pay their fines.

In December 1680 fines amounting to a colossal £9,680 were served on twenty-two Dissenting ministers, including Owen, Annesley and the second Edmund Calamy. In 1681 Benjamin Agas or Agus (1622-89) was fined £840 and Arthur Barham (1618-92), £600 for holding conventicles. Watts says that in October 1682 the informer John Hilton claimed to have obtained convictions that had cost the Dissenters in London and Westminster £17,000 in a period of only six months.

At this low point in the persecution years even the aged and fragile were abused. Baxter, who apart from a brief time in prison in 1670 had largely escaped persecution, was arrested for contravening the Five Mile Act and for preaching five sermons in 1683. His doctor testified that prison could kill him, so with the king's permission he was allowed his freedom 'that I might die at home'. But he says:

> They executed all their warrants on my books and goods; even the bed that I lay sick on, and sold them all.

In 1683 there was a plot, the Rye House Plot, to kill the king and his brother. This convinced the government or rather gave them an excuse to continue repressing Dissenters as a matter of national security. Baxter was again arrested on scurrilous charges for the sake of national security. Though just skin and bones by this stage he was cruelly and unfairly abused by the notorious Judge George Jeffreys (1645-89), who called him 'an old schismatical knave, a hypocritical villain' and recommended that he be flogged. Instead, he was found guilty of sedition and sent to prison.

## James II

When James II became king in 1685 he was the first openly Roman Catholic monarch since Mary. He shared her passion for Romanism but while pushing his own religion as far and as fast as he was able, he also conceived of a plan to extend toleration to Dissenters, as a way of uniting with them against the Anglicans.

In the wake of the failed Monmouth Rebellion in the west of the county, which did involve a number of Dissenters, James was able to get the Test Act and the penal laws repealed and free Baxter and many others from prison. Then, in 1687, he made a gracious declaration to all his loving subjects for liberty of conscience, stating that although he obviously wished everyone was a Catholic,

> ... conscience ought not to be constrained, nor people forced in matters of mere religion; it has ever been directly contrary to our inclination, as we think it is to the interest of government, which it destroys by spoiling trade, depopulating countries, and discouraging strangers, and finally, that it never obtained the end for which it was employed.

The last four reigns had sought to impose rigorous uniformity on the nation and palpably failed.

> For after all the frequent and pressing endeavours that were used in each of them to reduce this kingdom to an exact conformity in religion, it is visible the success has not answered the design, and that the difficulty is invincible.

How sincere James's belief in toleration was has long been debated.

Watts is confident that he 'broke the back of Anglican intolerance and made possible the permanent toleration of Dissent once William of Orange had landed'.

The repeal of the penal laws and Test Acts was a great relief to the Dissenters. Some eighty addresses thanking the king were presented by Dissenting churches and their ministers. However, it was all again done without the consent of Parliament and so did not have the status desired. The Presbyterian Daniel Williams (1643-1716) persuaded a group of London ministers not to present an address of thanks to the king, saying that 'it were better for them to be reduced to their former hardships, than declare for measures destructive of the liberties of their country'. Baxter and Kiffin were among those who supported him in this.

## The Glorious Revolution

In 1688 a son and heir was born to James and it was not long before the king was forced to flee the country, having alienated people on all sides. It is possible that his Romanism would have led to persecution of Dissenters eventually. Certainly, it is not until the nineteenth century that the sort of toleration envisaged by James became a reality.

What happened then was that an Act of Toleration was signed instead by James's daughter Mary and her Protestant husband William of Orange in 1689. William and Mary together became the new Protestant joint-monarchs. The act was a step back from what James had proposed but was not an act of arbitrary power nor a matter of mere short-term political expediency. At last a certain amount of pluralism under a Trinitarian, Protestant umbrella was to be allowed.

Despite his efforts William of Orange was not able to do as much for the Nonconformists as they had expected but he did introduce religious toleration for Protestants in the 1689 Act. The worst was now past, though many disabilities remained for Nonconformists.

The 1689 act marked the victory of Independency over Presbyterianism in that it was an act of toleration rather than of comprehension. Philip Henry, who had not previously held meetings in his house when there was preaching in the parish church, 'was at last prevailed with to preach at public time every Lord's Day' which he did for the rest of his life.

It also marked the end of what Watts calls 'the heroic age of Dissent'. In that period Dissenters had revealed their greatest qualities: 'their faith, their courage, their largely unwavering loyalty to God rather than the state'. Having kept their gospel coats on, as it were, through the stormy blasts of opposition, would they continue to do so in the sunshine of an easier day? Puritanism had always been a reformist movement; now it was, in Spurr's words, 'part of the spectrum of sects'.

It would be more than a century before Dissenters gained proper civil equality though the years. The necessity of receiving the sacrament as a qualification for office was eventually repealed in 1828 under George IV. All acts requiring the taking of oaths and declarations against transubstantiation were repealed by the Catholic Relief Act of the following year.

Meanwhile that first generation of Nonconformists was dying out. Goodwin died in 1680, Owen in 1683, Bunyan in 1688 and Baxter in 1691.

Gilbert Burnet, speaking to John Howe, suggested the movement could not last with its leaders all dying but Howe replied that he

> ... did not reckon it to depend upon persons, but upon principle, which when taken up upon grounds approved upon search, could not be laid aside by men of conscience.

As Owen testified before his death,

> I am leaving the ship of the church in a storm; but whilst the great Pilot is in it, the loss of a poor under-rower will be inconsiderable.

# 7 | THE FAREWELL SERMONS — 'FOR FEAR OF OFFENDING GOD'

One surviving feature of the Great Ejection of 1662 is the farewell sermons that were preached before men were silenced or removed from their pulpits in the parish churches. These sermons were mostly preached on the Sunday or sometimes the Sundays before 24 August 1662.

Some carefully prepared sermons for the press. In other cases, 'with the presence of many practised note-takers within the various congregations', there were also 'a substantial number of valedictions' available to the book trade. Sermons by the leading ministers soon began to appear first in pamphlet form. These were then gathered into books, licensed and unlicensed, that were also welcomed by the public. Even to this day some of these sermons are in print, especially a volume of twenty-four sermons by men such as Baxter, Calamy, Case and Manton.

Professor David Appleby is presently the man who has given most attention to these farewell sermons. In his informative academic work of 2007 *Black Bartholomew's Day* he argues that the sermons would have had an incredible impact in their day.

He says that some seventy-seven sermons by some fifty men were printed. There were also eight sermons by Moseley preacher Joseph Cooper (1635-99) amalgamated and printed together. We also have information about a number of valedictory addresses recoverable from various contemporary diaries and other similar accounts. Appleby draws attention to five sermons in manuscript form. The same hand transcribed sermons by the Westminster Divine Thomas Ford (1598-1674), Lewis Stukeley or Stucley (d. 1687) and Thomas Powel, delivered in Exeter. These have been preserved at the Bodleian Library in Oxford. Two sermons by Matthew Newcomen given at Dedham can also be found in Dr Williams's Library in London, one of which was published, though in a revised form.

The overwhelming majority of printed sermons appeared between 1662 and 1664. At least nineteen pamphlets of various sizes circulated, from one or two sermons to the fourteen-sermon series of Richard Fairclough (1621-82). As noted, compilations also soon began to appear, first by London men and then by those from elsewhere. At least sixteen compilations appeared between August 1662 and March 1663, some containing as many as forty-two sermons. There was at least one translation — into Dutch.

In 1633 a unique and anonymous East Midlands collection *England's Remembrancer* was published. Unlike other publications, it contained only farewell sermons, no funeral sermons or other materials. Calamy III revealed the names of the authors in 1713. Writers included John Whitlock (1625-1708) and Robert Porter (*c.* 1623-90).

We must remember that, all told, this is still only a small fraction of the hundreds of farewell sermons that must have been preached at the time.

In 1862 Robert Vaughan wrote of the sermons:

> Men who expected the Nonconformist pulpits to be charged with invective and bitterness on that day were disappointed. More than one volume of the sermons then preached is extant, and the general tone of the discourses is such as an apostolic spirit only could have dictated. The great aim of the preachers is to inculcate devout feeling, religious steadfastness, and conscientious integrity, with the special seriousness to have been expected from such men dealing with such themes, and in such circumstances.

## Jenkyn and Calamy

In most of the extant sermons direct reference to the ejection is minimal. However, the texts were carefully chosen. William Jenkyn, for example, preached in the morning on Hebrews 11:38 and observed that 'a godly man sees a very great worth and excellence in the people of God in the midst of all the trouble and persecution that can befall them'. In the afternoon he went to Exodus 3:2-5, taking the burning bush as a sign that the true church will continue despite its tribulations.

Calamy went to 2 Samuel 24:14. He says at one point that

> There are two sorts of straits in Scripture; some suffer for God and a good conscience, and there are straits suffered for sin.

On straits suffered for God and a good conscience he turns to Hebrews 11:36, 37 and says:

> Those martyrs there were driven to great straits; but these were straits for God and a good conscience, and these straits were the saints' greatest enlargements, they were so sweetened to them by

97

the consolations and supportations of God's spirit, a prison was a paradise to them, Hebrews 10:34. They look joyful at the spoiling of their goods, Acts 5:41. They departed from the presence of the council, rejoicing, that they were counted worthy to suffer shame for his name. Straits for a good conscience are greatest enlargements, therefore St Paul glorieth in his strait: Paul a prisoner, &c.

## Baxter

Baxter says little about the ejection but he does urge two lessons on his hearers — unnecessary divisions are to be avoided and no law of man can make it to be a duty to submit the soul to the direction of blind guides. 'But if our guides be taken away,' he imagines the people asking, 'what shall we do?' It is not the denial of public liberty that puts an end to the relation between a pastor and his flock, he answers, nor should any word from man cause a poor soul to trust itself for guidance of salvation to one that is not able. A man's soul is not to be hazarded by being deprived of the offices and ordinances of Christ and cast upon the 'conduct of a blind guide, for the pleasuring of a mere "man"'.

## Caryl

Joseph Caryl preached on Revelation 3:4 and again said little directly except:

> I would only say this to you, that as I have from this text, and many more, laboured to bring poor souls into a white state, to a state of justification, to a state of holiness; and as I have been pressing you to keep your garments white that you maybe in the habit of white, as your reward; so it shall be the desire and prayers of my heart, that if I should have no more opportunities among you, that as you have been stirred up to get into this white of grace, that you and I may meet in the white of glory, where we shall never part.

# Case

Coming at a slightly different angle, Thomas Case, also in Revelation, said:

My brethren, we have no great cause to boast of England's first love. Never so good as it should be, yet many can remember when England hath been much better than it is.

Time was, when doctrines have been more sound, discipline more exercised for the suppressing of sin and profaneness; ordinances kept more pure from sinful mixtures; when London kept sabbaths better than now, loved their godly ministers more than now, honoured them that were set over her for their works' sake, would have thought nothing too good for a faithful minister; when Christians loved one another with a dear, hearty, fervent love; when there was less compliment, but more real love and affection among Christians; when Christians improved their meetings, converse, Christian conference, and other soul duties to better purpose than now; not to foolish disputations, or wanton sensual excess, but to their mutual edification; when they improved their times for comparing their evidences, communicating their experiences, and building up one another in their most holy faith; when there was more industry in professors than now, to bring in converts; when private Christians thought it their duty to be subservient to the works of their ministers to bring in others to Christ, especially their family...

Time was, when more care of the truly godly poor; when error was more odious; when popery was more hated than now; when the name of a toleration would have made Christians to have trembled; when Christians were better acquainted with their bibles; when more time spent in secret prayer; when more tender of one another's names and honours, would heal one another's reputations...

Oh do you not only your first works, but our forefathers first works: be as zealous for God and his truths as tender, mutually careful of one another as they.

Our fears be very great, and truly our provocations be greater: our dangers are great, but our sins greater: yet here is a word, here is matter of encouragement, that yet there is balm in Gilead, physic of Christ's own composition, for the reviving and healing of a backsliding people.

Christians, Christ Jesus is become your physician, he hath prescribed you a potion made up of these three ingredients, self-reflection, holy contrition, thorough reformation. Christians, now take this receipt. Christ advises you, if you will not, there is no way but one, 'Or else I will come unto thee quickly, and will remove thy candlestick.'

There is yet a means or two I find in Scripture for the preventing of threatened ruin that hath been very near, that God hath prescribed for a people or person in great danger, when ready to be cut off and destroyed.

## Bates

William Bates, we have noted, said almost nothing in his two sermons of 17 August 1662. However, at the close of the second he did say:

> I know you expect I should say something as to my nonconformity. I shall only say this much. It is neither fancy, faction, or humour, that makes me not to comply, but merely for fear of offending God. And if after the best means used for my illumination; as prayer to God, discourse, study, I am not able to be satisfied concerning the lawfulness of what is required: if it be my unhappiness to be in error, surely men will have no reason to be angry with me in this world, and I hope God will pardon me in the next.

## Collinges

John Collinges said:

> I do fully close with him that said, No sober man will go against reason. No Christian against the Scripture: and no

peaceable-minded man against the church. But then the church must shine by a Scripture-light. If that be a rule, it must be ruled by the Scripture. The church's power is not authoritative, as to give laws against the laws of Christ; it is only ministerial. We do believe the Scripture for itself, and not because of the church; we receive the Scripture by the church. Hence, therefore, when we set up the name of a church, let us see whether that church walk in the way of Christ, whether she be his spouse or no, whether she doth act according to his institutions, — whether they bring his light, yea or no; then submit. For it is not what a church practices, but what they are warranted to practice: not what they hold for a truth, but what they are warranted to hold as the word of truth. The word was written after the church; but as it is the word of God, it is before it. This, therefore, will break the snare. If you be set upon by the specious name of the church, look that the church hath warrant from Scripture-institution, and then submit to church-institution.

## Hancock

Calamy summarizes the moving sermon by Edward Hancock of Bristol on 2 Corinthians 13:11 thus:

> At this time I am called to a work, which possibly may be unpleasing to many, even as to myself; that is, to die a civil death, whilst I am naturally alive. When the sun for this day is set, I shall then cease from having any charge over you, and you will then cease from having me to be your Minister. I may say as one did that was going to die a violent death, 'I am this day to do a work that I never yet did, I desire of God to give me strength that I never yet had.'

> Those that die well do usually these things:

> 1.  Make their Peace with God. I think I can give up my account with joy, in reference to the discharge of my duty, having kept back nothing from you of the counsel of God.

2. Die in perfect charity with all men. I hope I do so truly; having not the least thing against any man this day.

3. Set their house in order. You know I have made it my work for these two months past to show unto everyone his duty.

4. Give good counsel to their friends. I shall take up the greatest part of my time with counsel to you all, therefore attend to the last words of a dying man.

1. Consider the days of grace have their last. The day long threatened is now come, when my preaching and your hearing can be continued no longer: So all your comfort and joys will have an end.

2. Let us heartily bless God for so many years freedom, especially the last three, about which time I have been with you

3. Depart not from the truths you have received.

4. Let professors study to honour God.

5. Own God in your families. If no family prayer, expect no family blessing.

6. Sanctify the Sabbath.

7. Take heed of sinking under any sufferings. If persecution may come, we know not how soon our sins may deserve it.

8. Get all good from your minister, and do all good to your minister, that God shall set over you.

9. Study peace. There is no question but the nonconformists will be used rigorously, but be contented. It is like many may be come this day to catch words to entrap me. I beg and beseech you all, that you think of nothing, nor use any help to deliver yourselves out of sufferings, but faith, patience and

prayer. I profess before you all, I have not spoken with, nor heard of any of this persuasion, but they are all against having any hand in any war, even those who had a hand in the last; and therefore a horrible slander is cast upon the most peaceable subjects that God and earthly princes can have. I hope I shall never hear of any nonconformist that hath a hand in any rising or sedition whatever.

10. Be not troubled at the reproaches the enemies of God may cast upon you...

11. Learn how to behave yourselves well in the day of Jacob's troubles. (Have the mark of mourners on your foreheads; keep ... pure from the sins of the times ... feel the sorrows of the church; cry mightily unto God that he would have mercy...

12. Be truly wise (View Truth and study it; follow the light of it; practice self-denial ... live in the sight of, and dependence on, the Father, Son and Holy Spirit; live in a good air, keep good company; exchange temporal joys for eternal; fill thyself with religious pleasures; if thou lovest life, let death dwell in thy heart; conform to the terms of salvation, impartial dependence upon Christ ... never depart from faith and holiness I am going away and am not to speak any more unto you, except God find out a way beyond expectation. Great proffers of preferment formerly moved me not, but the terrors of the Almighty now make me afraid. My heart could not be strong, nor my hands endure in the day of the Lord, should I, against my conscience, have continued amongst you. I thank you all for your desire of me to stay: the Lord knows how loath I am to leave you, might I continue with a good conscience. I cannot say more; the sun is even down; my civil life is near an end; my strength is almost spent.

Farewell sermons, farewell sabbaths, farewell fastings, farewell exhortations, farewell this house, farewell this seat for ever, farewell my preaching, farewell your hearing, and farewell your faces in this place. Farewell this world, when we shall arrive at eternity, both old and young. My brethren and Sisters all, farewell!

## Jacombe

Thomas Jacombe said relevantly:

Comfort will not be wanting to those who conscientiously endeavour to please God. The comfort lies in this, — you may suffer, but the Father will not leave you alone. Pleasing God does not secure a man against suffering from man. Sometimes, it rather exposes a man to suffer from men. But though it does not prevent suffering, it takes away the sting and venom. It makes it to be like Samson's lion when it was slain, in which he found nothing but honey. Pass a charitable interpretation upon our laying down the exercise of our ministry. There is a greater judge than you, who will judge us all at the great day; and to this judge we can appeal before angels and men, that it is not this thing, or that thing, which puts us upon this dissent.

It is conscience towards God, and fear of offending him. I censure none who differ from me, as though they displeased God. But yet, as to myself, should I do thus and thus, I should certainly violate the peace of my own conscience, and offend God, which I must not do; no, not to secure my ministry, though that is, or ought to be, dearer to me than my very life. How dear it is, God only knoweth. Do not add affliction to affliction. Be not uncharitable in judging of us, as if through pride, faction, obstinacy, or devotedness to a party, or, which is worse than all, an opposition to authority, we do dissent. The Judge of all hearts knows it is not so.

## Lye

Thomas Lye (1621-84), ejected from All Hallows, Lombard Street in London, went into some detail. He said:

104

There are secret ordinances: it may be thou canst not be so much in the pulpit as thou wouldst. Oh! be more in thy closet. It may be thou shalt not have so many opportunities to hear so many lectures: be more conscientious in thy meditations in secret. It may be thou shalt not have that freedom with God in public: be more earnest with God in private.

Mind your families more than ever. You have your children and servants calling loudly upon you. Let the Amorite, Peresite and Jebusite do what they will, but for you and your children, and your servants, do you serve the Lord. When we cannot hear a sermon, then read a sermon. If we cannot hear a sermon well preached, godly parents should read sermons well penned. If nothing new, let the word repeated and meditated call to mind what you have heard. Let the debauched atheists know they have something among you to be feared — that is, your prayers. Let them know that, if you have not the opportunities you have had, you will improve those you have.

He imagines people asking what pious people are to do when ordinances and a faithful ministry fail them. He answers:

Wherever Christ finds a tongue to speak I am bound to find an ear to hear. I would not be mistaken. I bless God I am not turned out of my ministry for being a schismatic, nor know I any of my brethren that are so. But this I would advise — I speak as though I were dying — do whatsoever lies in your power to hear such men as you think to be godly. Beg of God, be earnest with him that he would give pastors after his own heart, and whom God hath sent: not such as may daub with untempered mortar, and not such as may prophecy lies in the name of the Lord; not such as may be clouds without water, but such as may be guides of the blind, burning and shining lights, faithful stewards. What shall you do? What did you twenty or thirty years ago? What did the good old Puritans do? They were not schismatics. But as much as lies in you possible, hear them whom in your conscience God doth hear. Oh! then expect the word of God should come to your hearts, when you have ground to believe it comes from your pastor's heart. I must confess, I intend to do the same, when put into the same condition with you. I acknowledge I am bound in conscience to hear the word of God, but I must take care whom I hear, hear those by whom God speaks. I hope God will grant several such...

Thus I have now spoken something from this Scripture. I cannot speak what I desire; for besides the exhausting of my spirits, there is something to be done after, viz. a funeral sermon. I shall say no more, but only this: the God of heaven be pleased to make you mind these plain things. I can truly say this, I have not spoken one word that I remember, which I would not have said to you if I had been a dying, and being to go to God as soon as gone out of the pulpit, and the God of peace be with you. Only mind that one thing, 'when God doth not find a tongue to speak, do not you find an ear to hear, and a heart to believe.'

## Slater

The London minister Samuel Slater (1629?-1704) closed his sermon with these words:

I suppose you all know, there is an Act come forth by Supreme Authority, and it is not for us to quarrel at all, but to submit to it, and hold correspondency with a good conscience; and there being many injunctions, that many, besides myself, cannot comply withal, therefore we are willing to submit to the penalty inflicted.

This I say, you have for many years had the benefit of my poor labours; I have fulfilled near up towards forty years, and have performed my service to God, Christ, and his people, and I bless his name, not without acceptance and success. My work, so far as I know, in this course, as in the weekly course, is now at an end; my desire is, that you whose hearts have been inclined to wait upon God, in the way of my ministry, may be kept faithful to God, and that you may have the blessing of the everlasting covenant coming upon your souls, and that you may have the power of this doctrine, held forth in this sermon, put forth upon your hearts; that as ye do believe that Jesus is the Christ, that Jesus is the Son of God, that as you profess these things, you may carry it suitably to your profession, that you may walk in love to God, love to Christ, and love to one another; that you may labour to manifest a noble, generous spirit in overcoming the world in errors, corruptions, false doctrines, and unwarrantable worship; that you may in all things labour to approve yourselves: and, little children, keep yourselves from idols. Amen.

## Prayers

Another feature of those momentous times are the farewell prayers that were also taken down in some instances. To give just two examples. GN (probably George Newton) prayed in this way:

To thee, O Lord Jesus, we commend ourselves: To thee who judgeth rightly, thy poor servant resigneth, and committeth this congregation. The Lord pardon unto me wherein I have been . wanting unto them: The Lord pardon unto them, wherein they have been wanting in the hearing of thy Word, that we may not part with sin in our hearts. Unto thee who judgest uprightly I commend them. The Bishop of Souls take care of them: Preserve them from the love of the World: teach them to wait on thee, and to receive from thee whatever any one or family may stand in need of.

Provide them a Pastor according unto thine own will, only in the mean time give us that anointing [that] shall lead us out of our own wills and ways, that we may walk in the ways of Christ Jesus. The Lord Jesus say now amongst them, I am your Shepherd, you shall not want. Say to them as thou didst to thy disciples, Let not your hearts be troubled, you believe in the Father, believe also in me. So far as we are able we put thy Name upon them: we name the Name of the Lord Jesus over them. The Lord Jesus bless them; teach them to follow holiness, peace and a heavenly conversation. The Lord make them useful to each other. The Lord Jesus be a blessing to them, and me and all ours. The God of Peace and Consolation fill them with blessings according as thou seest every one stand in need of. To thee, O Lord, we commend them, do thou receive them, that under thy counsel they may be preserved blameless, until the day [of] Jesus, where we may all meet crowned with glory. Amen.

Thomas Jacombe prayed like this:

Blessed God, thou art a God blessed for ever; thou givest mercy to all returning and repenting sinners; thou art worthy to be praised by all that draw nigh unto thee.

Thou hast vouchsafed to us one Sabbath more; Oh that we might all of us be in the spirit upon the Lord's day, that whatever we do, we may do it in the strength of God, that we may offer spiritual sacrifices to God this day, through our Mediator the Lord Jesus.

It is a very great condescension, that thou shouldst suffer such as we are to come unto thee; O Lord, we are unclean, we are unclean, from the crown of the head to the sole of the foot, we are overspread with the leprosy of sin; all the faculties of our souls are defiled; our understandings are darkened; our wills are corrupted; we have affections but they are carnal; we have hearts, but they are impure; we have consciences but they are seared: and as our inward man, so our lives are unholy; as the fountain is, so is the stream: besides that, our general guilt that we brought into the world, we are guilty of innumerable actual transgressions against thy holy Law: We think, O Lord, there are no greater sinners in the world than we; our sins are attended with many aggravations.

We have sinned against prayers, against vows and promises; we have had as much light shining before us, as any in the world have had: great is our unbelief. Oh that we could lay these things to our hearts! ...

O Lord, we are thine own work, but we are dead in trespasses and sins; give us grace, and speak a word to them that are dead; put out thine Almighty Power, and draw some sinner to Christ this day; and those that have any breathings after thee, Oh! Thou that gavest them that desire, carry on thine own work in them; where thou hast begun a good work, carry it on; let sin, as the house of Saul, grow weaker and weaker, and grace, as the house of David, grow stronger and stronger: Oh! Increase our faith; O Lord at this time we do not only stand in need of grace but of a great measure of grace. Oh! Help us by faith to rely upon God, that thou mayest help us at last: Bless with us all thine; remember thy people from one end of the world to the other: Thy people are very low; this is a time of Jacob's troubles, the Bush is burning every day. Oh thou the Hope of Israel and the Saviour thereof! Show thyself in mercy to these nations. We bless thee for all thy mercies, that thy judgments do not seize upon us every day, that thou dost not sweep us away, that thou dost not rain fire and brimstone on England as thou didst on Sodom: our sins cry aloud to heaven for vengeance: God is greatly provoked every day, and it is a miracle of patience that thou hast not destroyed us. God can pardon the sins of the nation at once; but we are not fit for pardon; we do not humble ourselves; O Lord, humble us, give repentance to England from the highest to the lowest that we may return unto thee.

We desire to bless thee, that our enemies have not had their wills over us: they said, they would pursue and overtake, and satisfy their lusts, but God did blow upon them, and they did sink in the mighty water and thou hast yet preserved thy church; we pray thee do not leave us, nor remove thy gospel, whatsoever thou dost.

Pour down the choicest of thy blessings upon our Sovereign Charles by thy Grace, of England, Scotland, France, and Ireland. Bless him with the blessings of Heaven and Earth; make him a blessing to all of us: Bless him in all his relations; the Lords of the privy Council. Look on them that have desired an interest in our prayers, known to thee are all of them; know their souls in this time of adversity; make their beds in their sickness: Give faith to them that complain of unbelief: give the Spirit of Prayer to those that complain they cannot pray: be a Counsellor to those that want counsel in their affairs, either by sea or land, let thy blessing go with them wherever they go: Spare the lives of children if it be thy will.

Prepare us for thy good and holy Word, let it be a savour of life unto life, and let it come with power unto us. Oh let us hear it as thy Word, not as the word of a poor man, but as the Word of God; and all for the Lord Christ his sake; for whom we bless thee; to whom, with thee and the Spirit of Grace, be given Glory and Honour for evermore.

## Legacy

As David Appleby points out the farewell sermons were never at any point 'imbued with an iconic status remotely comparable to Foxe's memorials of the Marian martyrs'. What gave Nonconformity its character rather was 'the vicissitudes of persecution and toleration' and 'social, cultural and religious discourse within and between the nonconformist communities themselves'.

The farewell sermons were a feature of this. 'Nothing preserved the vision of a Bartholomean nucleus', however, says Appleby, like the efforts of those early historians that led eventually to Calamy's memorials. Those memorials make scant reference to the sermons, probably because even at the time when they were appearing opposition to such sentiments was still strong.

Thankfully, there are still those today who have an appetite for such preaching and are willing to read the farewell sermons where they are available. They may never reach the stature of Foxe or of Bunyan's *Pilgrim's Progress* but as testimonial to the faithfulness of their authors and as sermons in their own right they should continue to have a place in the thinking of those who seek to serve God today.

# 8 | 'THEIR NAME LIVETH FOR EVERMORE' — THE EJECTED MEN, WHO WERE THEY? (PART 1)

I remember going on a trip to the Continent during secondary school and being taken to visit the war graves in Dunkirk, where you can see almost endless lists of names of men who lost their lives in the Second World War. For a twelve-year-old it was not the most exciting afternoon of the trip, though the very numbers of names could not fail to impress. Older, and perhaps wiser, I might appreciate such an experience a little more today. This chapter and the next function very much as a 'war memorial' as they seek to list the names of at least some of the hundreds and hundreds who for the sake of conscience suffered in those far-off days.

There were some two thousand men ejected altogether in 1662. Inevitably there was a certain variety among them. For some, ejection came towards the end of their ministries, while others were only at the beginning. Some we might have expected to have been ejected — such as Reynolds; Lightfoot; the author of *The Christian in Complete Armour* William Gurnall (1617-79); or the commentator John Trapp (1601-69) — conformed. Some too, perhaps, were ejected who one might have expected to have conformed. This question of conscience was no easy one to decide. Some who were ejected later conformed; some who conformed were later ejected.

Some had always been comfortably well off, others had not been or were not from that point on. Some faced great opposition at this time, some less. According to A. G. Matthews a hundred or so had 'considerable private means' to fall back on. Among the rest, 101 kept schools (nine led ministerial academies); fifty-nine practised medicine; forty-seven became chaplains to the nobility or gentry; ten became farmers; nine went into trade.

As for the ejected, though many are today unknown, some names are still remembered. In a nineteenth-century work the author Robert Halley spoke of

> ... the preaching of Baxter, the theology of Owen, the genius of Howe, the learning of Goodwin, the reasoning of Charnock, the sermons of Bates, the devotion of Flavel, the meditations of Isaac Ambrose, the expositions of Matthew Poole, the labours of Oliver Heywood, the life of Joseph Alleine! ... It is not for me to praise the men who have done much to make old England what it is: a great, a free, a glorious, a strong, a religious, a Protestant country. They have left their deep and indelible impressions upon the history of our land, and upon all its institutions...

We have already mentioned eight of the ten men named by Halley, omitting only two — the warm and godly Lancashire author Isaac Ambrose (1604-64), whose books were admired for their pathos and beauty even by those with no sympathy for Puritanism, and the Bible commentator Matthew Poole (1624?-79), who, fearing a Popish plot against him, fled to Amsterdam, where he died shortly after.

The *Oxford Dictionary of National Biography* (ODNB) currently considers just over two hundred of the ejected men worthy of attention. We have already referred to about fifty of these in the body of the book and in this chapter and the next we will list some more. We have also mentioned twenty or so not listed in the ODNB, namely Barham, Bell, Chambers (aka John Grimes), Cole, Collins, Cooper, Cromwell, Farroll, Fownes, French, Hancock, Herring, Hieron, Hoppin, Hughes, William Jones, Littlejohn, Pell, Powel, Stukeley or Stucley, John Thompson, John Turner, Henry Williams and Richard Worts.

## Individuals A-H

As for those in the ODNB, if we focus first on the letters A-H, we have already mentioned the following: Agas (Agus), the Alleines, Alsop, Ambrose, Annesley, Bates, Baxter, Bury, Clarke, Collinges, Corbet, Delaune, Firmin, Flavel, Ford, Gouge, Hardcastle, Henry and Samuel Hilders[h]am.

Edmund Calamy (1600-66), WD, whose son Edmund Calamy (1634-85) was also ejected. Their son and grandson Edmund Calamy III (1671-1732) later did much to preserve the story of ejection. Plus Richard Fairclough, the son of Samuel Fairclough (1594-1677) and brother of Samuel Fairclough (1625-91), also both ejected; Oliver Heywood, whose brother Nathaniel Heywood (1633-77) was also ejected; Independent Joseph Caryl, famous for a long series of sermons on the Book of Job now back in print and Presbyterian Thomas Case, WD, a published author and well-respected preacher.

To these add:

## A

The brothers Richard Adams (1626/7-98) [Ox] and Thomas Adams (1631/2-70) [Ox] ejected 1662. Thomas, a published

113

author, should not be confused with others of the same name.

Henry Albin of Somerset (1624-96), who was 'of a large acquaintance and a very friendly temper' and 'had a majesty in his countenance, and yet was clothed in humility' (Calamy). L. 1672 (Presbyterian).

Thomas Allen (1608-73) [Cam] the Norwich-based author of a book on chronology that uses Scripture to calculate that Jesus's death was 3,968 years after creation. Deprived for refusing to read BS 1636, he was ejected 1662. L. 1672 (Independent).

Devonian Bartholomew Ashwood (1622-78) was the son of an Anglican father and the father of a Nonconformist son, all ministers. He was silenced 1660 and imprisoned 1662. L. 1672 (Independent). Three books appeared posthumously, one with a preface by Owen.

Yorkshireman William Aspinwall (d. 1702) [Cam]. L. 1672 (Presbyterian). He is sometimes confused with author William Aspinwall (1602-73) [Ox], also ejected, and William Attersoll (d. 1640), father of another ejected minister, William Attersoll (1590/91-1664).

# B

John Ba[t]chiler/Bachilor (d. 1674) [Cam, Emmanuel] was ousted 1660. Ox. Oath 1666.

Thomas Baldwin (d. 1693) [Cam] was Baxter's assistant and successor. L. 1672 at his own house.

Nathanael Ball (*c.* 1623-81) of Somerset [Cam, King's] was a diligent minister and scholar in various places. L. 1672 (Presbyterian). Sadly, his scholarly manuscripts and large correspondence are lost to posterity.

John Bartlet (1599-1680) [Cam] and older brother William Bartlet (1609/10-82) [Ox, New Inn], both published authors,

114

were based in Devon. John was a college friend of Sibbes. L. 1672 (Independent) but arrested with many others the next year. 'A very laborious constant preacher' with 'an excellent copious gift in prayer' (Calamy). John Rogers referred to William alongside Ames and Ainsworth as one of the 'champions of the church'. He was also imprisoned for Nonconformity.

Thomas Baylie (1581/2-1663) of Wiltshire [Ox] was a fellow of Magdalen 1600-15 and possibly later a Fifth Monarchist. WD.

Suffolk-born, John Beadle (1595-1667) [Cam] was indicted for refusing to read BS 1633. He is best known for his 1656 tract *Journal or Diary of a Thankful Christian* on Numbers 33:2.

Cumbrian William Benn (1600-81), a moderate Puritan, was complained against for long-winded sermons and little Prayer Book use in the 1630s. He opposed BS 1634 and in the 1640s was fiercely anti-Royalist. Ejected 1662. L. 1672 (Independent). His daughters married ejectees — Theophilus Polwhele (*c.* 1626-89), Hugh Thomson (b. 1604) and Nathaniel Mather (1630-97).

Robert Bennet[t] (d. 1687) [Cam] was ejected from Waddesdon, Buckinghamshire. L. 1672 (Presbyterian). He was a chaplain to Philip, Lord Wharton (1613-96) and wrote a concordance.

Kent-born John Billingsley (1625-83) [Ox, Exeter]. After ejection in 1662 he established a Dissenting academy in Mansfield. L. 1672 (Presbyterian).

Derby-born classical and oriental scholar John Bingham (1612/13-89) [Cam] was a schoolteacher and assisted Brian Walton with the 1657 Polyglot Bible. Despite considerable enticement from lifelong friend Sheldon, he felt unable to conform 1662. He would attend the parish church in the morning and preach at his own house in the afternoon until excommunicated.

Samuel Birch (1620/21-80) [Ox] younger brother of politician John. After his ejection in 1662 he ran a school and was a chaplain to Lord Wharton. It was said that fourteen MPs in one parliamentary session of Queen Anne's time had been his pupils. He was constantly harassed by magistrates. L. 1672 (Presbyterian) in his own house.

Published author John Bisco[e] (1605/6-79) [Ox] of High Wycombe. Ejected from Abingdon 1660, he moved back to Southwark but was driven from there to Uxbridge. L. 1672 (Independent) at his own house.

William Blackmore (1616-84) [Ox, Lincoln]. This rigid Presbyterian was involved in the earlier attempt to restore Charles II and implicated in Christopher Love's plot, nearly losing his London pastorate. Ejected 1662, he began a conventicle in Hornchurch, Essex. L. 1672 (Presbyterian).

Samuel Blower (d. 1701) went to school with Howe. He had 'a meek temper, peaceable principles, and a godly life'. (Calamy)

Pomeranian Mauritius Boheme or Bohemus (*fl.* 1646-62).

Matthews tells us that there were 132 father and son pairs ejected, including two sets of synonymously named fathers and sons: James Bradshaw Sr (1613-85) [Ox], James Bradshaw Jr (1635-1702) [Ox, did not graduate] of Bolton and John Brinsley Sr (1581-1624) [Cam], John Brinsley Jr (1600-65) [Cam, Emmanuel] of Ashby-de-la-Zouch, Leicestershire.

Andrew Bromhall (1608-62) [Ox, Balliol] must have died very soon after the Act of Uniformity was passed.

Town preacher at Ipswich, Benjamin Brunning (1623-80) [Cam], chose Nonconformity — unlike his father, brothers and son — and moved to St Clement's parish, where conforming friend Samuel Golty succeeded John Ward (brother of Samuel, a predecessor of Brunning). Golty died April 1662, escaping Brunning's dilemma.

John Bryan (d. 1676) [Cam, Emmanuel] was brother to Jarvis

(Gervase) Bryan, twenty years his junior, also ejected. After 1662 Presbyterian John Bryan attended services in the established church as a layman and preached to other Nonconformists. Some of his sermons were published.

Daniel Bull (1633?-97/98) was an assistant to Howe after his ejection but sadly fell into adultery, perhaps unique among the ejected.

John Burgess (1622/3-71) [Ox] ministered in Devon until his ejection. Thomas Brooks was his son-in-law, according to Calamy.

Edward Burghall (1600-65) of Acton, Cheshire, a school teacher and minister, is best known, Palmer says, because he left a manuscript called 'Providence improved; being remarks taken from his Diary' (1628-33).

Richard Byfield (1598-1664) [Ox], half-brother of Puritan author Nicholas Byfield (1578/79-1622), was suspended for not reading the BS 1634. WD (he replaced Daniel Featley [1582-1645]). Buried in Mortlake church, a brass plate says he 'painfully and constantly taught and kept the Word of God and the Testimony of Jesus Christ' in thirty-five years as Long Ditton Rector.

Cornelius Burges[s] (d. 1665) [Ox] WD and Anthony Burges[s] (d. 1664) [Cam, Emmanuel] WD were unrelated but both had Watford connections and were published authors.

# C

Thomas Calvert (1605/6-79) [Cam], a Hebraist and published author, ejected 1662, was subsequently banished from York, gaining asylum at the house of Lady Barwick, near Tadcaster. He later returned to York and lived quietly there until his death.

Daniel Cawdr[e]y (1587/88-1664) [Cam] WD. Opposed BS 1633. His father was ejected 1588 for opposition to the Prayer Book. A published author and a strong Presbyterian, he was ejected 1662.

Oxford-born Francis Cheynell (1608-65) [Ox] WD was a well-connected religious controversialist who opposed Socinianism, Arminianism and the Seekers. Baxter considered him one of the 'over-Orthodox doctors'. In 1647 he wrote 'the Mysterie of Iniquitie works highest in Dr Sheldon, who is the eldest son of Prince Lucifer'! He gained a doctorate 1649 and was Lady Margaret Professor of Divinity at Oxford but resigned from the post.

Nicholas Clagett (1610-62) and his colleague Samuel Slater were ejected March 1661. Hoping to continue in the established church they obtained licences August 1661 from the Bishop of Norwich, Edward Reynolds. Clagett's sons, William and Nicholas, became eminent Anglican divines. Some 158 sons of ejected men took Anglican orders.

Matthew Clarke (c. 1630 - c. 1708) [Cam] contested attempts to displace him 1660 but was eventually ejected 1662. After this he 'preached to his friends in private houses, as long as he had opportunity, but the persecution growing hot' he moved to a house in Leicester Forest. He was eventually prosecuted and imprisoned three times. By 1672 he led one of the country's largest congregations at Market Harborough. He was later fined and had goods seized. A very learned man, he kept his preaching plain and accessible.

David Clarkson (1622-86) [Cam] was Owen's last assistant and successor in London.

William Cooper (fl. 1640-81) was one of ten ejected men who moved to the Netherlands. He spent several years in there as chaplain to the Queen of Bohemia. A Presbyterian representative at the Savoy Conference, he was ejected 1662. Ox. Oath 1666. L. 1672 (Presbyterian) in Somerset, where he had gone after his ejection. He was one of the Dissenters imprisoned during the 'Tory reaction' 1681.

Bolton-born John Crompton (1611-69) [Cam, Emmanuel] was

unsympathetic to the interregnum government but was none-
theless ousted from his pastorate in Derbyshire 1660 and ejected
from one in Nottinghamshire 1662. Calamy refers to a published
farewell sermon no longer extant.

Devon-based William Crompton (1630/33?-96) [Ox] was ejected
1662. In his final years he must have been very poor as he received
a grant from the Common Fund (1690-96). He wrote tracts on
prayer, superstition and other matters.

Scot Francis Crow (1627-92/93) ministered in East Anglia before
and after his ejection. He was in the West Indies between 1686
and 1690.

Richard Culmer (c. 1597-1662) [Cam] was suspended for refusing
to read BS 1634. A strong Puritan, in 1643 he gained notoriety by
breaking images and windows in Canterbury Cathedral. Ejected
1660, he died March 1662.

## D/E

Londoner Thomas Danson (1629-94) [Ox] was ejected 1661 but
found a new living in Suffolk, only to be ejected again. He spent
the rest of his life preaching in London or Abingdon. L. 1672
(Presbyterian) at his own house. Later he moved to Abingdon
— his connection there being another ejected minister turned
physician, his father-in-law Tobias Garbrand (d. 1689). Danson
was excommunicated and taken to court for not attending church
1684. He wrote against Quakers, Socinians, Papists, Hobbists and
the 'hypothetical universalism' of Howe (Baxter complained he
should have been the target) Marvell wrote against Danson in
order to hinder 'one Divine from offering violence to another'.
He returned to London 1692. BF.

William Dell (d. 1669) [Cam, Emmanuel], a published author
(popular with Quakers) and an educational reformer was master
of Gonville and Caius (1649-60). In the 1640s he was chaplain

to Sir Thomas Fairfax and the New Model Army. Keen on unity he rejected uniformity, emphasizing heart religion. He often tangled with Presbyterians who, probably justly, accused him of antinomianism. Parishioners complained 1659 as he had not celebrated communion at Christmas and let Bunyan the tinker preach (typical of his conviction that learning does not make a preacher). Ejected from his Bedfordshire pastorate early 1661 he spent his final years in retirement.

Yorkshireman Nathan Denton (1635-1720) [Ox] was ejected 1662, refusing other offers of preferment. L. 1672 (Presbyterian). He gained the right to use his house as a place of worship 1689. He received a grant from the Common Fund (1693-1720). By 1713 he was 'the picture of an old puritan' and led 'an unblameable life, and maintained his integrity' (Calamy). He lived longest of all the ejected. His son Daniel also became a minister.

Timothy Dod (d. 1665) [Cam, Emmanuel], son of the famous Puritan John Dod (1550-1645), studied under Ames at Leiden. He served in Daventry at first though he was in London 1644-46. A famous and oft repeated story says he became so fat in later years that he could not mount the pulpit so had to preach from a pew or behind a desk. Ejected August 24 1662, he saw his wife buried two days later. He became ill with gout and other ailments and died three years later.

Thomas Doolittle (1630/33?-1707) [Cam] was a well-known Puritan minister and author. Born in Kidderminster, he was converted through Baxter's sermons later published as *The Saints Everlasting Rest*. Baxter arranged for him to study at Pembroke College, where Richard Vines (1600-55/56) was master (1644-1650). He became a successful London minister. J. William Black notes that he 'had a pregnant wife and three small children when he decided against accepting the terms for conforming' 1662. He opened a boarding school in Moorfields, later taking on Thomas Vincent as assistant. This is where Vincent was during the plague. On returning to London, Doolittle opened a meeting-house and was often harassed. L. 1672 (Presbyterian). He set up an academy in Islington. He was forced to move out 1673 but returned. He was fined £40 in 1682 and knew a peripatetic existence as he sought to escape fines. After 1689 his academy was London's 'leading Presbyterian academy'. Calamy and Matthew Henry were pupils. BF.

Thomas Douglas (d. *c.* 1684), ejected 1662, left the country owing to a scandal. He became a physician and later moved to Ireland.

William Dyer (1632/33-96) was a man of 'great piety' and 'a serious fervent preacher' (Calamy). Little is known of his early life but he became a popular writer on Christ's titles and the plague, his collected works appearing 1668. He was buried as a Quaker.

Richard Eedes (1610-86) [Ox] served in Gloucestershire. A Presbyterian, he liked Baxter's ideas on unity. Despite hopes of some sort of dispensation he was silenced 1662. Some of his sermons were published.

# F

John Fairfax (1623/24-1700) [Cam] was ejected 1662 along with his father Benjamin Fairfax (1592-1676) and uncle Nathaniel Fairfax (1637-90). John maintained himself and his family through farming and the help of wealthy benefactors. He preached Matthew Newcomen's funeral sermon 1669 and the next year he was arrested with others for Nonconformity and spent more than five months in prison. L. 1672 (Presbyterian). Throughout the 1680s and '90s he continued his ministry, preaching 'seven times in a fortnight, besides frequent "occasional sermons"'.

Lancastrian Henry Finch (1633-1704) was active in the 1659 Royalist rising under Sir George Booth and was fined. Ejected 1662, he was later forced to move to Manchester, where he supported himself by keeping a school and rarely preached. L. 1672 (Presbyterian). As he began to preach more he was imprisoned in

Chester during Monmouth's rising 1685. He provided corrections to Calamy's original account of ejected ministers 1702.

Samuel Fisher (1605/6-81) [Ox], not to be confused with a Quaker of the same name, was based mainly in Shropshire and Cheshire. Hostile to the regicide and the regime that brought it about, he seems to have settled at Birmingham after his 1662 ejection. L. 1672 (Presbyterian).

Devon-born Thomas Ford (1598-1674) [Ox] WD was a fellow of Magdalen Hall before entering the ministry. An anti-Laudian sermon preached in Oxford 1631 got him in trouble. He later served on the Continent before settling back in England, where he preached before Parliament and published sermons. Back in Devon he sought to establish an association on Baxterian lines. He remained in Exeter after the Restoration, preaching a farewell sermon 13 August 1662. After 1665 he retired to Exmouth, where he wrote more. L. 1672 (Presbyterian) in his house in Exeter but died 1674.

Wiltshire-born Christopher Fowler (1613/14-77) [Ox] was a zealous Calvinist and Presbyterian based in Reading who was ejected 1662. He began a conventicle and was ordered to be sent to Windsor Castle but cannot have been detained long. L. 1672 (Presbyterian) in Surrey (but not in Reading).

Birmingham-born Timothy Fox (1629/30-1710) [Cam, Christ's] served in Staffordshire before and after his 1662 ejection. L. 1672 (Presbyterian) at his own home. He spent time in jail 1684 and at the time of the Monmouth rebellion the next year. His house in Cauldwell, Derbyshire, was certified as a place of worship 1689. He preached in many places.

Unlike brothers Thomas and Samuel, Francis Fuller (1636?-1701) [Cam] refused to conform 1662. Ordained by his uncle Thomas, Bishop of Ardfert and later Archbishop of Cashel, he became an itinerant preacher after ejection, alternating between London and the west, especially Bristol and Bath. L. 1672 (Presbyterian) at Bristol. In 1695 he became assistant to Timothy Cruso

(1657-97) in London. His very practical works were later praised by Nonconformist Job Orton (1717-83). At his funeral Jeremiah White (1629-1707) called Fuller a 'downright honest Englishman'.

According to a monument at his Norwich meeting-house Martin Fynch or Finch (1628/29-98) [Ox, Trinity] 'laboured abundantly in the ministry of the gospel 49 years, and guided this church of Christ 12 years with great wisdom and integrity, diligence and faithfulness'. He ministered in Lincolnshire until his ejection 1662, after which he served in Norwich, where he faced persecution from time to time. L. 1672 (Independent). Later he returned to Lincolnshire though by 1685 he was back in Norwich, where he died.

# G

Theophilus Gale (1628-79) [Ox] adopted the Independency and Calvinism of Goodwin and Owen while a lecturer at Magdalen Hall. At the Restoration, he lost his university post and became tutor to the sons of Lord Wharton. He established an academy in London for Dissenters' children and assisted John Rowe (1626/27-77) at an Independent church. He eventually succeeded Rowe alongside Samuel Lee (1625-91). A lifelong bachelor, he left money to Goodwin and Owen and for an education trust for needy Nonconformist ministerial candidates. His writings appeared 1669-79. Several were devotional, some biographical (on Rowe and Thomas Tregosse) and one was on Jansenism. His reputation as a theologian is based on his monumental four-volume *The Court of the Gentiles*. Very Platonic, based on a reading of Grotius, it argues that all truth and knowledge derive from the ancient Jews. This is a form of what is called Euhemerism. BF.

Allan Geare (1622-62) was educated on the Continent before taking up a London charge that came to an end only because of ill health. He eventually ended up back in his native Devon, working alongside Flavel. Ejected August 1662, he was dead by the year's end, possibly from influenza.

Thomas Gilbert was the name of at least two ejected men. Thomas Gilbert (1609/10-73) may have been of Scots origin. He was ejected 1661 and, like 14 other ejected men, emigrated to New England, where he died. Thomas Gilbert (1613-94) [Ox] of Shropshire was ejected 1662 and took in as boarders sons of Nonconformists who went to Magdalen School, undertook tasks for Lord Wharton and continued to preach in Oxford. In 1664 Owen and others may have proposed him as president of Harvard. Gilbert felt that even if worthy of such a post he ought rather 'at present to frame myself to suffer in Old, than to reign in New England'. L. 1672 (Independent). He seems to have suffered little harassment for his Nonconformity until the 'Tory reaction' 1681. Happiest with a partial or semi-conformity, he wrote on many subjects. Anthony Wood calls him 'the common epitaph-maker for dissenters'.

Philip Goodwin (d. 1667) was a published author from 1649 on practical subjects, including a book on dreams. He was ejected from Watford June 1661 and died a few years later.

Robert Gouge (1629/30-1705) [Cam, Christ's], father of Thomas Gouge, refused to conform 1662. In 1672 he moved with his sons from Ipswich to Coggleshall in Essex to pastor a Congregationalist church. Some sermons were published.


# H


Thomas Hall (1610-65) [Ox] was the older brother of conforming Calvinist Edmund Hall (1657-87). First a school head but from 1632 a minister, he became a polemicist and debater, writing against long hair and on various other subjects. C. D. Gilbert calls his works 'an amalgam of populist and erudite writing'. In a manuscript he wrote of Cromwell 'with considerable warmth and considerable regret' seeing the Restoration as a disaster. After his ejection he lived in great poverty. His bachelor house became 'a kind of puritan seminary for young ministers'. He left his library to what became Birmingham Central Library. 'A dedicated minister, a successful teacher, a passionate (and at times acerbic) controversialist' he 'fought all his life against popular revels and pastimes'. He 'could inspire devotion in pupils, fellow ministers and parishioners'.

Self-taught West Countryman Joseph Hallett I (1620-89) was ejected 1660. L. 1672 (Presbyterian) at Exeter but imprisoned the following year. Between 1673 and 1687 he was fined a total of £120 for preaching and was again imprisoned 1685. His health was badly affected by prison and he began to have fits and mental health problems. His eldest son, Joseph, continued his work in Exeter.

Samuel Hammond (d. 1665) [Cam] was ordained 1642 and ended up in the north-east. He opposed the Quakers and the Baptists at Hexham who had blotted their copybook in the case of the False Jew. Unwilling to conform 1662, he sailed to Hamburg, where he ministered to the expatriate community. Clarendon's opposition to this led to a move to Stockholm then Danzig. In 1665 he settled briefly back in England at Hackney, preaching occasionally in his own house.

George Hamond (1619/20-1705) [Ox] was educated at Trinity, Dublin, then served in Devon and Dorchester. Though ejected, he managed to stay on until March 1663. Ox. Oath 1665. L. 1672 (Presbyterian). In 1677 he became co-minister with George Newton in Taunton and also opened a boarding school. Newton died 1681 and the meeting-house was wrecked by order of the mayor 1683. Following the Monmouth Rebellion Hamond was forced to flee to London, where he ministered alongside Richard Steele (1629-92). 'A man of great learning, exemplary piety, and an admirable temper; but not valued and esteemed according to his worth' (Calamy).

Jonathan Hanmer (1606-87) [Cam, Emmanuel] was another Devonian. A moderate Presbyterian, he wrote in favour of restoring confirmation and on the early church fathers. He left several unpublished manuscripts, and letters to him reveal his support for missionary work among New England Native Americans. His wife died 1660 and he was ejected 1662. He continued to preach when possible in Devon, Bristol and London, gathering a congregation in Barnstaple. L. 1672 (Presbyterian). His son became a Presbyterian minister, his daughter Katherine was mother to the poet John Gay.

John Harrison (1614-70) [Cam, Emmanuel] probably studied at Trinity, Dublin, as well as Emmanuel. He became one of a circle of devout Presbyterians in Manchester. Like many Presbyterians he deplored the regicide. He was imprisoned 1651 with others on suspicion of having entered into correspondence with Charles II and again in 1659 for his involvement in a plot to restore the monarchy. Ejected 1662, he was arrested for preaching the following year and the next came under suspicion of plotting against Parliament. His friend Henry Newcome called him 'a precious man of God, learned, sound, zealous and pious, one that feared God above many, and suffered much in many ways with great courage and patience'.

Published author Thomas Harrison (1617/18-82) [Cam] spent some time after 1640 ministering in Virginia but was banished 1648 for sitting loose to the Prayer Book. By 1650 he was back in England opposing Arianism and Socinianism with Nye, Owen and others. In 1655 he travelled to Ireland with Cromwell. By 1661 he was in England and was ejected from Chester 1662 and imprisoned for preaching the next year. In 1665 he was again arrested, fined and imprisoned. L. 1672 (Presbyterian) in Chester but soon returned to Dublin. Daniel Williams (1643-1718) preached his funeral sermon. Lord Thomond once expressed a preference for hearing Harrison say grace over an egg over any prayers or preachings of bishops.

Richard Hawes (1603/4-68) [Cam] was educated in Ipswich (under Samuel Ward [1577-1640]). Losing his childhood faith he 'for many years after he entered into the ministry ... continued much addicted to vain company, and was sometimes guilty of excessive drinking' but was brought to his senses when he almost died at Hereford, during its garrisoning in the Civil War. He was imprisoned at the Restoration. As a moderate, he was expected to conform 1662 but refused and was ejected. He continued to preach.

Gaspar Hickes (1605-77) [Ox] WD served in Cornwall. Ejected 1662, he continued to preach and at some point after 1670 was prosecuted. The Justice in his own district refused to convict him so he was taken further west, where he was fined £40. L. 1672 (Presbyterian).

Yorkshire-born rebel John Hickes (1633-85) was educated at Trinity, Dublin, and served briefly in Ireland before moving to the West Country. Ejected before November 1660, he was one of six Dissenting ministers living in Saltash, Cornwall, 1665 but had to move with the passing of the Five Mile Act. He married a daughter of Howe and anonymously chronicled the persecution in Devon and Cornwall 1671. Having been charged with murder after a magistrate died, allegedly as the result of forcibly dispersing a conventicle in his house, Hickes went into hiding for about six months 1670/71. He and others were pardoned by the King, January 1672. He spent most of that year in London expediting the obtaining of licences for hundreds of men. L. 1672 as was his house. He also persuaded Charles to remit a third of the fines levied on Dissenters in the West for holding conventicles. He wrote about his experience of persecution again 1673. He was executed at Glastonbury 6 October 1685 for his part in the Monmouth Rebellion. He assured his wife he died for defending Protestantism and English liberties.

The controversialist Henry Hickman (1629-92) [Cam & Ox] was a good friend of Baxter. A voluminous polemical writer, he sometimes used a pseudonym, Theophilus Churchman. At the Restoration he lost first his post as vicar of St Aldates, Oxford, then, in 1662, his university fellowship. He went to the Netherlands and served the church in Leiden with Newcomen but had to return to England to answer charges concerning his conduct before the Restoration. Back in England, he worked as a tutor then opened a school. In 1688 he appears to have founded a library at Stourbridge Grammar School. He returned to Leiden 1674 and studied for a medical degree.

Martin Holbe[a]ch (1597-1670) [Cam] studied under John Preston (1587-1628) and came to know Cotton and Hooker. For many years a school teacher in Essex, he became a minister of increasingly Independent viewpoint who was ejected 1662.

Francis Holcroft (1628/9?-92) [Cam] shared a room with John Tillotson (1630-97), later Archbishop of Canterbury, as a student, which was when he adopted Puritan principles. Ejected 1660, he began to preach but was imprisoned in Cambridge for illegal preaching 1663. Eventually released, he carried on preaching and was imprisoned again in the Fleet, where he kept on preaching. In and out of prison through the '70s and '80s, he latterly became depressed by 'the headiness of some of his people, who turned preachers, or encouraged such as did so'.

George Hopkins (1620-66) [Ox], minister at Evesham and the son of a man described by Baxter as 'the most eminent, wise, and truly religious magistrate of Bewdley', his own son was the conforming antiquary Dr William Hopkins (1647-1700). He was ejected 1662. Ox. Oath 1665.

John Horne (1616-76) [Ox] served in King's Lynn from 1646 until his ejection. A published author, he was very sympathetic to universal redemption. Like Baxter and Amyraldus he believed in general redemption and indeed went beyond them in that his universalism was not hypothetical. Cited 1661 for disregarding the Prayer Book, he was ejected 1662. He attended the parish church and had a universalist conventicle. L. 1672 (Presbyterian). His generosity was legendary in Lynn, where he died 1676.

Charles Hotham (1615-72) [Cam] ministered in the north of England before becoming a fellow at Peterhouse. He wrote poetry and several philosophical tomes, being a disciple of mystic Jacob Boehme (1575-1624). In the early 1650s he ran into trouble with the government chiefly over how Peterhouse was being run (under Lazarus Seaman [d. 1675]). He was deprived of his fellowship and returned to parish ministry. He was able to retain the rectory of Wigan at the Restoration but was ejected 1662 for Nonconformity. In 1668 he was elected to the Royal Society. Early in 1670 he and another man, William Edwards, were appointed ministers to Bermuda, where he died 1672. His will required his astrological books to be burned 'as monuments of lying vanity and remnants of the heathen idolatry' but bequeathed his astronomy books to the public library in Bermuda.

George Hughes (1603/4-67) [Ox] ministered in Oxford and London until being suspended by Laud 1636, accused of refusing to use the sign of the cross in baptism and not bowing to the altar. He contemplated emigration but was persuaded to stay by John Dod, who obtained a chaplaincy for him with Lord Brooke at Warwick Castle. He later ministered in Devon and was at the sieges of Exeter and Plymouth. He was a leading light among the Devon ministers and some of his sermons were published. At the Restoration he was recommended for a bishopric by Baxter but was ejected 1662. His popularity did not wane and he continued to preach. In 1665 he and Thomas Martin, his brother-in-law and assistant at Plymouth, were arrested and imprisoned for nine months in such severe conditions that he developed dropsy and scurvy. When friends paid a £2,000 security without his knowledge he was released. A daughter married Howe.

Scot Abraham Hume (1614/15-1707) served in chaplaincies in Scotland and London, travelling to Paris and Geneva. In 1643 his employer Lauderdale was one of five Scottish commissioners to the Westminster Assembly and Hume came south with him. This led to ministry in the north of England. Ejected 1662, Hume returned to the household of Lauderdale, who urged him to conform. His determined refusal eventually led to a breach. He was in France 1669 but returned to London to minister. L. 1672 (Presbyterian). His congregation disintegrated and he had to leave London at one point but returned and carried on preaching into his nineties. He died at the age of 92. BF.

John Humfrey (1621-1719) [Ox] was long lived, a prolific writer of tracts, a friend of Baxter and of no particular party. He ministered in Somerset from 1654 until his 1662 ejection. Many of his views were not typical of the ejected. For example, he objected to any doctrinal test for those wishing to take the Lord's Supper and saw it as a converting ordinance. He also opposed both

Commonwealth and Protectorate and made no secret that he sought the return of Charles II. Invited by the restored Bishop of Bath and Wells to assist in ordinations 1660, he was re-ordained but then renounced it and ended up publishing both for and against re-ordination. He then moved to London and preached there. He considered taking the Oxford Oath 1669 but seems not to have. He remained a man of no party in Nonconformity and sought continually to achieve the union of English Protestantism and toleration for Nonconformists. L. 1672 (Presbyterian) at his own house in Kingsbury but jailed the following year for a tract promoting comprehension. He was also fined for illegal preaching 1682. His defence of toleration extended even to antinomians and he was almost as liberal as Baxter on justification. Also like Baxter, he sought a middle way between Calvinism and Arminianism. A seemingly endless series of tracts on comprehension of moderate Nonconformists continued as well as his preaching until late in life. Of all the ejected only Nathan Denton outlived him.

Henry Hurst (1629-90) [Ox] ministered in his native Gloucestershire and in London until his ejection 1662. After 1662 he continued to preach in various places. By the late 1660s he was at Mickleton, Gloucestershire, and took up chaplaincies to the Countess of Manchester 1674 and the Earl of Anglesey 1677. He also provided a commentary on Ezekiel as part of the continuation of Poole's Annotations on the Bible. He was a certified preacher in Lincoln's Inn Fields, London, 1689 but the next year suffered an apoplectic fit during a sermon and died the next day.

(Key: [Ox] or [Cam] reveals that the man attended Oxford or Cambridge University; 'BS' = 'Book of Sports'; 'WD' = Westminster Divine, a member of the Westminster Assembly; 'Ox. Oath' means he took the Oxford Oath, the demanding oath required to escape the rigours of the Five Mile Act; 'L. 1672' means the man was licensed to preach by the indulgence of that year. 'BF' means he was buried in Bunhill Fields, London.)

# 9 | 'THEIR NAME LIVETH FOR EVERMORE'— THE EJECTED MEN, WHO WERE THEY? (PART 2)

## Geographical distribution

In an appendix we give a county by county list of ejected ministers. David Appleby comments that 'religious dissent was everywhere in evidence'. He notes that Richard Greaves found Presbyterians to be strongly represented in Northumberland, Lancashire, Cheshire, Devon, Somerset (especially Bristol) and Carmarthen in South West Wales, while Congregationalists proliferated in South and Central Wales, the Midlands, Essex, Suffolk and Lancashire.

A. G. Matthews thought that the concentration of Nonconformist ministers was highest in the West Country, followed by Essex, Suffolk and Lancashire, with a fairly even distribution elsewhere.

This West Country predominance is noticeable in the printed literature. London also, unsurprisingly, dominates with sixty men. The phenomenon was found in every county, facilitated by various efficient networks.

## Youthfulness

Appleby also tells us that by the mid-seventeenth century the average clergyman began ministering in his mid-twenties and commonly went on for another thirty years. Seaver says that between 1640 and 1662 the average age of incumbents rose to forty-two. Appleby says that the average age at the ejection of those listed by A. G. Matthews (where the data is available) was 41.9 years. The average from those who published farewell sermons is 39.6 years. Ten Midlands authors featured in *England's Remembrancer* were on average aged as low as 32.7 years. The point then is that far from being past their prime, those ejected in 1662 were younger than average.

Even the older ones could be very energetic. Appleby cites Richard Fairclough (41) who habitually rose at 3 a.m. to squeeze in all the various things he did in a day. This factor should be borne in mind when we consider how it was that most of these men (unlike the elderly bishops recently restored) went on preaching for decades after 1662.

## Education

Though not all university men, those ejected in 1662 were well educated and trained in rhetoric, often using Latin, Greek and even Hebrew to get the message across. Non-university men like Richard Baxter and John Oldfield were clearly well read, which was a Puritan tradition. Appleby makes the point that 'Far from being inferior, the ejected ministers of 1662 were at the very least the intellectual equals of the conformist clergy.' They were educated not just in their college days but afterwards through household seminaries run by experienced ministers. From the time of Elizabeth, godly conferences had been a feature of the scene. Those such as the one at Dedham had become famous. They have been compared to modern professional associations.

## University men

Appleby also says that despite statements by W. F. Mitchell in 1932 saying that those who were ejected were generally poorly educated, some eighty-five per cent were university graduates. Most (733) had gone to Cambridge, especially those who had farewell sermons printed.

At least eighty-seven attended Emmanuel College, 'a hotbed of Puritanism'. Appleby suggests that the tutors would have encouraged friendships among the students and that men like Ralph Venning, George Swinnock and John Whitlock (all of whom graduated from Emmanuel 1646) would have known one another from their teenage years, being part of a larger group of Puritans that included other colleges. Luke Cranwell, Henry Newcombe, John Barrett, Robert Seddon and Oliver Heywood all graduated from Cambridge that same year. Fewer (513) had studied at Oxford but just four colleges — Exeter, Magdalen, New Inn Hall and Wadham — produced 111 Nonconformists between them. The writers went to Wadham (Robert Adkins, Thomas Lye, Thomas Manton) and Exeter (Joseph Caryl, John Galpin, George Newton). Another 34 had studied Harvard, Dublin or one of the Scottish universities.

## Individuals L-Z

To resume our alphabetical list, already mentioned in the body of the book are these:

Ince, Jackson, Jacombe, Jenkyn, Jollie, Lawrence, Newcomen, Newton, Norman, Porter, Quick, Slater, Spurstowe, Daniel Williams and Thomas Watson. We have also mentioned Thomas

Vincent whose younger brother Nathaniel Vincent (1637/38-97) was ejected too.

To them we add:

## L

John Langston (1640/41-1704) was ejected from Gloucestershire 1660 and eventually ministered in Ipswich. L. 1672 (Independent) in London.

George Lawrence (1613-91/98) [Ox, New Inn] was anti-Royalist and probably spent the Civil War as an army chaplain. He pleaded for toleration for the plotter Christopher Love but failed. A London minister then a hospital chaplain in Winchester, he was ejected 1660 but continued to preach in London.

Based in Essex but in France at the Restoration, silenced minister Henry Lukin (1628-1719) [Cam] was 'of great note and eminence … a judicious and learned divine' (Calamy). L. 1672 (Independent). A friend of John Locke, he wrote several books on practical subjects such as prayer and faith.

## M

Presbyterian John Machin (1624-64) [Cam] of Cheshire was 'a worthy instrument in gospel work. Laborious, faithful and successful above his fellows, taken away in the midst of his days' (Matthew Henry). Converted from a dissolute youth, he became a generous-hearted Christian. A great friend of Henry Newcome (1627-95) and Thomas Leadbeater (1627-79), he used his ancestral estate near Newcastle under Lyme for Christian gatherings. Intense and a rousing preacher, he had a habit of carving texts on trees, walls or mantelpieces of homes he visited. Ejected 1662 he came home and died two years later.

Thomas Mallory (d. 1689) [Cam] from Northamptonshire, not to be confused with a Royalist Cheshire clergyman of the same name, was a London preacher who had among his hearers the diarists Bulstrode Whitelocke (1605-75) and John Evelyn (1620-1706). In 1653 Evelyn recorded that though 'somewhat of the Independent, yet he ordinarily preached sound doctrine, and was a peaceable man; which was an extraordinary felicity in this age' and in 1657 heard him preaching against Fifth Monarchists. He was ejected 1662.

William Manning (1630/33-1711) [Cam] like his brothers, John and Samuel, was a Suffolk clergyman. All three were ejected at the Restoration. Sadly, William later turned Socinian and denied Christ's deity, a very rare example of such a thing among the ejected.

Walter Marshall (1628-79) [Ox] ejected 1662 became an Independent minister in Hampshire. L. 1672 (Independent). It is reported that he was continually troubled by an unquiet conscience and consulted Baxter about it. His *Gospel Mystery of Sanctification* was published 1682 and has been in print ever since.

Welshman and published author Marmaduke Matthews (*c.* 1606-83) emigrated to New England in the 1630s but returned home 1654 to minister in Swansea. Ejected 1662 he still 'preached, by the connivance of the magistrates, in a little chapel at the end of the town' (Palmer). L. 1672 (Independent). 'A very pious and zealous man', he 'went about to instruct the people from house to house' (Calamy). His three sons became Nonconformist ministers but later conformed.

Sussex-born gentleman John Maynard (1600-65) [Ox] WD. He preached before Parliament and was a published author. Ejected 1662, he was married some four times, not unusual in those days.

London and Kingston minister Richard Mayo (*c.* 1630-95) continued to preach following his ejection 1662. L. 1672 (Presbyterian). About 1689 his people built him a new meeting-house in Salters' Hall Court. He published books on prayer, unity and other matters. His youngest son Daniel followed him at Kingston and Hackney.

Bedfordshire-born Matthew Mead[e] (1628/29-99) [Cam] was a well-known London minister who knew Baxter and worked with William Greenhill. After ejection, he continued to preach. Perhaps the most famous of his many works is *The Almost Christian Discovered* (1662). He spent some time in the Netherlands but returned and was often arrested and fined and his goods were distrained though he was never in prison. Following the discovery of the Rye House Plot he fled the country again. On returning, after Owen's death in 1683, he became lecturer at Pinners' Hall and devoted his final years to the cause of Nonconformist unity. Richard Greaves calls him 'an uncompromising Nonconformist for nearly four decades, … deeply concerned for Protestantism's future in England. His support for Monmouth, his enthusiastic embrace of William, and his efforts on behalf of Nonconformist unity were manifestations of that concern'.

Suffolk-born John Meadow[e]s (1622-97) [Cam, Emmanuel], brother of diplomat Sir Philip, was ejected 1662, having been ordained five years before. L. 1672 (Presbyterian) in Stowmarket. In 1675 he married second wife Sarah Fairfax (1654-88), daughter of Benjamin Fairfax (d. 1708), a granddaughter and niece to three ejected ministers mentioned in the previous chapter. He eventually lived in Bury and was an occasional conformist. He often used part of his considerable wealth to assist needy Independent and Presbyterian ministers.

According to Calamy, Luke Milbourne (1622-68) was a Presbyterian Royalist, which earned him abuse from Parliamentary soldiers, an interview with their general and a narrow escape from imprisonment. He kept 30 January, the date of the king's execution, as a fast day for the rest of his life. Ejected 1662 this Midlands pastor moved to Coventry and did not preach. The authorities prevented him from taking boarders for the grammar school. He later moved to Newington Green, near London, where his wife kept a school.

Somerset-born John Milward (1619/20-80/83) [Ox, New Inn] urged his people, May 1660, to show themselves men and fight 'for I do believe too many of us have popes in our bellies. Let us fear the king of heaven and worship him, and be not so desirous of an earthly king, which will tend to the embroiling of us again in blood'. It was November 1661 by the time he was ejected.

Thomas Mocket (*c*. 1602-70) [Cam] was a controversialist and a published author from Kent. He wrote against excesses at Christmas, among other things. Opposed early in his ministry, he moved west to Wales but in the time of Cromwell, who he supported, was in Hertfordshire. Little is known of his later years.

Richard Morton (1637-98) [Ox] was ejected 1662 and, like others so ejected, he followed a career in medicine becoming an authority on tuberculosis and a fellow of the Royal College.

George Moxon (1602-87) [Cam] sailed to New England 1637, where he became a minister and prospered. He returned to England, however, and worked alongside Machin 1652. Ejected 1662, he preached at a remote farmhouse to evade the Five Mile Act. L. 1672. He seems to have become unorthodox later. His son was a Unitarian.

## N

Presbyterian James Nalton (*c*. 1600-62) [Cam] died shortly after his 1662 ejection. Previous to that he had served in various charges. He was implicated in Christopher Love's plot 1651 and fled to Rotterdam, where he ministered for six months before returning. Resolute and devout, he was described at his funeral by Thomas Horton (d. 1673) as someone who was known as 'the Weeping Prophet' since he was 'a man of a very yielding and melting form of spirit, soon dissolved into tears'.

Benjamin Needler (1620-82) was an Oxford fellow until marrying Mary, daughter of Cambridge Platonist, Nathaniel Culverwell (1619-51). A London Presbyterian minister, published author and a preacher at the Cripplegate morning exercises, he was ejected 1662. 'A very humble, grave, and peaceable divine' (Baxter).

We have mentioned Henry Newcome [Cam] above. He and his son Henry Newcome (1645-1713) were ejected 1662. Another son, Peter, conformed. Newcome Senior was a preacher in Congleton, then Gawsworth, both in Cheshire, then Manchester. Against the regicide he published the sermon *Usurpation Defeated and David Restored* in 1660. While decrying its frivolity he genuinely hoped for good things from the Restoration but was disappointed. He continued as much as he could to act as a parish priest after his ejection, even when forced to move from Manchester. L. 1672 (Presbyterian). He appears to have remained for many years a partial or occasional conformist, drawing criticism from both sides. Catherine Nunn says he 'deplored the disruptive effect of strife surrounding religion, and blamed hardline episcopacy for driving Presbyterianism towards Separatism. Although ejected, he remained on good terms with friends who conformed.' By 1689 he seems to have reconciled himself to being a Nonconformist. Several sermons were published before he died in 1695.

Ferdinando Nic[h]olls (1597/98-1662) [Ox] began his ministry alongside John White (1575-1648) in Dorchester then ministered in Devon. Ejected September 1662 he died before the end of the year. 'At his burial in the chancel on 17 December there was a disturbance from over a hundred objectors protesting at the service's being according to the prayer book.'

## O

Harvard-educated New Englander Urian Oakes (*c.* 1631-81) returned to England 1654 where he ministered both before and after his ejection in 1662. In 1671 he recrossed the Atlantic, later becoming president of Harvard, then still small but full of potential.

Converted through Samuel Hammond as a student, the Midlands preacher Henry O[a]sland (1625-1703) [Cam] was much influenced by Baxter. Ejected 1662, he had spent several months before that in prison on suspicion of involvement in a Presbyterian rising. He broke with Baxter 1670 over how to handle the prevailing situation. L. 1672 (Presbyterian). Some twelve sermons were preached at his funeral! He was 'a key member of the Worcestershire Association of ministers in the 1650s, and … after 1662, a Nonconformist preacher in the heroic mould', according to C. D. Gilbert, who notes that 'his spiritual autobiography (which deserves to be far better known) offers a remarkable insight into the mentality of a seventeenth-century puritan'.

Lancashire-born Samuel Ogden (1627/28-97), who ministered in Derbyshire 'thought the idolising the Common Prayer, and placing all religion in it, was a provocation to the good spirit of God' and was ejected 1662. He continued to preach. L. 1672 (Presbyterian). He was something of a Renaissance man with regard to learning but 'being of a melancholy disposition, and apt to be incumbered with troublesome fears about dying, it pleased God he was on a Lord's day seized with a palsy, as he was in the pulpit' and died a few weeks later (Calamy).

Derbyshire Presbyterian John Oldfield (1626/27-82) was brother-in-law to fellow minister Robert Porter. After their ejection in 1662 Oldfield wrote of his Nonconformity as below. He was later quoted by the Unitarian Elizabeth Gaskell, drawing on Theophilus Lindsay, in Chapter 4 of her novel *North and South*. Oldfield wrote:

> When thou canst no longer continue in thy work without dis-honour to God, discredit to religion, foregoing thy integrity, wounding conscience, spoiling thy peace, and hazarding the loss of thy salvation; in a word, when the conditions upon which thou must continue (if thou wilt continue) in thy employments are sinful, and unwarranted by the word of God, thou mayest, yea, thou must believe that God will turn thy very silence, suspension, deprivation, and laying aside, to His glory, and the advancement of the Gospel's interest.

His sermon 'Stumbling at the Sufferings of the Godly' appears in the collection *England's Remembrancer*. Jim Benedict says he

... expected the profane multitude to hail the ejections as well-deserved retribution, above all for the presbyterians' obnoxious attempts to restrict access to the sacrament. But it stung to hear even the godly whisper about their pastor as 'an ignorant, scrupulous, or obstinate fool'. Though it looked indeed as if God had 'spit in our faces', Oldfield reminded his hearers (and himself) that Christians were called to a life of suffering; besides, he added with more gusto, providence would eventually vindicate the godly ministers. He also defended his reluctance to submit to reordination and his refusal to accept ceremonies he deemed not only unedifying, but positively forbidden in scripture.

## P/Q

Thomas Pakeman (*c.* 1614-91) [Cam] worked as a proofreader in the king's print house then ministered in the south-east, something that he continued to do after his ejection. He escaped prison but was fined at least once. He worked as a tutor and preacher with former Gresham College professor Ralph Button (1601/2-80) and merchant Erasmus Smith (1611-91). His funeral sermon was preached by Richard Kidder (1634-1703), soon to be Bishop of Bath and Wells.

Published author Anthony Palmer (1616-79) [Ox] of Bourton-on-the-Water, Gloucestershire, was at the Savoy House Conference 1658 and became an Independent after being ill treated 1660 and fleeing to London with Carnsew Helme (*fl.* 1622-90). Both were known to be against the Restoration powers and were ejected 1662. Another Anthony Palmer (1613-93) was a member of the Devon Association 1655 and was ejected by October 1662. L. 1672 (Presbyterian).

Bolton-born Robert Parke (1600-68) [Cam, Emmanuel] spent several years in the Netherlands but ministered in his home area until his ejection in 1662. A friend of Newcome, Oliver Heywood preached his funeral sermon.

London-born Presbyterian Thomas Parson (1631 - *c.* 1668) [Cam, Pembroke] studied under Vines and was ejected 1662. E. C. Vernon writes that 'the parish vestry seems to have parted on good terms with him, paying him an advance on money owed and appointing a committee to collect the tithes owed' by parishioners. He ministered in Dublin after 1667. Calamy says he also helped Francis Gouldman (*c.* 1607-88/89) prepare his Latin dictionary.

Edward Pearse (*c.* 1633-73) [Ox], not to be confused with Edward Pearse/Pierce (1631-94) who wrote against Nonconformists, ministered in Westminster. After his 1660 ejection little is known about him. He may have lived at or near Hampstead, Middlesex.

Devonian William Pearse (1626-91) [Ox] was ejected 1660. L. 1672 (Presbyterian). Constant harassment led to a spell in London, where he was imprisoned for preaching. He later returned to Devon.

Henry Pendlebury (1626-95) [Cam] became 'one of the patriarchs of Lancashire dissent' and even before his silencing at the Restoration preached far and wide. In 1670 he was reported to the privy council for disturbing the reading of the service at Gorton Chapel and proceeding to preach. L. 1672 (Presbyterian). He later had a meeting-house next to his residence. 'A man of great learning and strict godliness' (Matthew Henry). Some of his sermons and some other practical works were published posthumously.

Suffolk-based Samuel Petto (*c.* 1624-1711) [Cam] was ejected 1660 and moved to Norfolk, where he continued to minister. L. 1672 (Independent) in his own house and another. From 1669 he was based in Sudbury. People complained that 'Mr Petto the Nonconformist preacher in the barn' was unmolested, only once having been brought before the quarter sessions, and then not punished. Greatly respected by Dissenters in the district, at his death he was buried in the churchyard of All Saints, Sudbury.

Pembrokeshire-born bilingual preacher Peregrine Philips (1623-91) was a supporter of Cromwell. He possibly led a gathered church in the late 1640s, though working within the national church until his ejection in 1662. From then on he was closely watched by the authorities and occasional imprisonment, repeated house searches, arrests and fines became the pattern of his life. Charged with holding religious meetings 1663 and 1669, both cases led to prison. L. 1672 (Independent). Stephen Wright says 'Though willing to suffer privation for his religious beliefs, Philips continued eirenic in his outlook' and 'took no small pleasure in reconciling differences' (Calamy). In June 1691 the Common Fund voted him £5 a year but he died that September.

Lavenham-born Abraham Pinchbecke (1626-81/82) [Cam] entered the ministry, becoming an assistant to Manton at St Paul's, Covent Garden, by 1657. He corresponded with Baxter for some time and, like him, was ejected.

London-born John Poynter (1600-84) [Ox] was 'devoted ... to the ministry from the womb' by his mother (Calamy). After a BA he studied under Dod then under Ames in Leiden with Dod's son. He served in various places until 1660 when he was obliged to resign and, as far as is known, never preached again.

# R

Essex preacher Nathanael Ranew (1602?-77) [Cam, Emmanuel] was ejected 1662. He was the author of the 1670 book *Solitude Improved by Divine Meditation*.

Yorkshire-born Presbyterian Christopher Richardson (1619-98) [Cam] was an intimate friend of Oliver Heywood, who began an unfinished biography. He ministered at Kirkheaton until his ejection in 1662. In 1661 he bought Lascelles Hall where he continued to preach after 1662, using the staircase as a pulpit 'so as to enable him to escape in case constables should come in to apprehend him for holding a conventicle'. His sons were educated with Heywood's. Second wife Hephzibah was the daughter of another ejected man Edward Prime (*c.* 1626-1703). From 1687 he began to preach often in Liverpool, where he died in 1698.

John Robotham (d. 1664?) [Cam, Emmanuel] was a minister mainly in London, being Caryl's assistant at one point. He authored many books from 1647 on. He was an admirer of Cromwell.

Probably the great-grandson of the martyr John Rogers and father of Presbyterian minister Timothy Rogers, John Rogers (1610-80) [Ox] ministered in several places but mainly in County Durham until his ejection in 1662, after which he still continued to preach. L. 1672 (Independent).

Somerset-born Thomas Rosewell (1630-92) [Ox] was apprenticed first to the silk trade but then began to prepare for the ministry. Though a Royalist, he was ejected 1662 but continued to minister in Wiltshire. L. 1672 (Presbyterian). In his later years he suffered with depression. His fame rests on his sensational trial for high treason 1684 before Judge Jeffreys, when three informers claimed he had spoken against the king. (On hearing of it Charles is said to have exclaimed: 'What! was so many at this conventicle and could none hear this treason but these three women?') He was found guilty but pardoned the following year. He caught a chill at Baxter's funeral in 1691 and died a little while after. BF.

A published author, John Rowe (mentioned in the previous chapter) [Cam & Ox] kept a diary in Greek from his youth but seems to have deliberately destroyed most of it in the months before he died. He began his ministry in Witney from where he published *Tragi-comoedia, Being a Brief Relation of the Strange and Wonderful Hand of God, Discovered at Witny*. It relates a tragedy that occurred as parishioners were staging a scurrilous and blasphemous play locally and is followed by three sermons on repentance and an end to such pursuits. He moved on to Devon then London and was very much part of the Cromwellian establishment. Despite his efforts when the Restoration came in he was ejected and became an Independent minister in Holborn. As stated, he was assisted then succeeded by his cousin Theophilus Gale. BF.

The seaman's preacher John Ryther (1631/35-81) was Yorkshire-born [Cam]. He entered the church, only to be ejected 1662. He continued to preach and for this spent several months confined in York Castle. On release he moved to London and started an Independent church for seamen. Arrested 1670, he was able to escape. He became a popular author, his works including sermons aimed at seafaring folk and a funeral sermon for his friend James Janeway. His son became an Independent minister and ships' chaplain.

# S

Nottinghamshire-born Henry Sampson (c. 1629-1700) [Cam, Pembroke] was stepson to Obadiah Grew (1607-89), also ejected. Sampson was displaced 1660 and ejected from his college fellow-ship. He studied medicine in Padua and Leiden and was made an honorary fellow of the Royal College 1680. He sat under Lazarus Seaman's ministry. A historian of Dissent, at his death his collection of materials was broken up and some parts lost.

Wiltshire-born Gabriel Sangar (1608-78) [Ox, Magdalen] was a fellow pupil with Clarendon in Gillingham, Dorset. Imprisoned at Salisbury for refusing to read BS 1633, he served mainly in Wiltshire before becoming rector of St Martin-in the-Fields 1653, where morning exercises were organized and later published with a preface by his friend Case (1656). Friendly with the Restoration authorities he was eventually ejected May 1663. He only escaped arrest 1665 because of the plague. He moved around in London and its borders frequently and had wealthy protectors. L. 1672 (Presbyterian) in the Strand.

Stephen Scandrett (1631?-1706) [Cam] 'spent several years in hard study, to fit him for the ministry, to which he was from the first inclined, never entertaining thoughts of any other employment' (Calamy). A chaplain at Trinity he was forced out at the Restoration and went to labour in Suffolk, for which he was perse-cuted and spent time in jail. L. 1672 at the house of Joseph Alders, which adjoined his own at Haverhill. He received a grant from the Common Fund (1690-92).

The eminent Lazarus Seaman (d. 1675) [Cam, Emmanuel] WD was born in Leicester and ministered in London. He was part of the Puritan brotherhood from an early date and became master of Peterhouse, Cambridge, 1644. He opposed the regicide but openly preached submission to and acceptance of the Commonwealth at Cambridge as well as London, for which he was pitilessly attacked in a pamphlet *Lazarus's Sores Licked* (1650). The year before he had become a DD, apparently the thesis being on the timely subject of 'the providence of God in disposing of political government'. President of Sion College 1651-52 and vice-chancellor of the University, 1653-54, his mastership of Peterhouse was strongly opposed 1658-59. In London he was unusual in trying to co-operate with Independents and Baptists. In 1660 he was ejected from Peterhouse and in 1662 from the ministry of All Hallows, Bread Street. His farewell sermon spoke of peace, especially 'that *inward* peace that we enjoy, if our conscience hath been troubled with terrors of sin, wrath, &c'. In this spirit he later persuaded Baxter to refrain from publishing a statement against taking the oath under the Five Mile Act 1665. He lived mostly in Hammersmith, Middlesex, after his ejection. L. 1672 (Presbyterian). He had a meeting place in Holborn.

Northamptonshire-born John Sheffeild or Sheffield (d. 1680) [Cam, Peterhouse] served in several places before coming to St Swithin, London, from where he was ejected 1660. Ox. Oath. L. 1672 (Presbyterian) in three places in Enfield, Middlesex. His books include *A Good Conscience the Strongest Hold*, 1650, the preface of which speaks of conscience as 'the book of books, the ancientest piece of scripture in the world' and laments how 'these times of ours have been too fruitful in disputes and controversies; in dealing with which there is no end'.

Nottinghamshire-born William Sherwin (1607-90) [Cam] was ejected 1660 and gave himself to writing, chiefly expounding millenarian doctrines, convinced that the Second Advent was imminent. These writings ceased abruptly in 1676.

John Shuttlewood (1632-89) [Cam, Trinity] was displaced from one living 1660 and ejected from another 1662. He became an active Nonconformist minister and was reported for this. He worked with Matthew Clarke in south-west Leicestershire but was often troubled by informers. Imprisoned 1669 he was later fined £20. L. 1672 (Presbyterian) at his own house near Market Harborough. Opposition continued even after his worst persecutor Charles Gibbons died December 1675, after drowning in a ditch where he had fallen returning home drunk one night. He eventually moved to Northamptonshire, conducting one of the earliest Nonconformist academies at Sulby, near Welford, from the late 1670s. His few students include Thomas Emlyn (1663-1741). An only son John Shuttlewood (1667-1737) was minister of an Independent church in London. His youngest daughter married Thomas Gibbons (1720-85), tutor at Homerton Academy.

John Stalham (d. 1677) [Cam, Christ's] was born in Norfolk and served in a place called Terling, which with the help of the Mildmay family and others he made a godly centre to which others were attracted from elsewhere in the county of Essex. While Laud held power he was often investigated for irregularities but with the changing scene he felt able to throw over the Prayer Book (which he denounced as an idol) and adopt an extemporary form of Puritan worship. From 1645 he was often away preaching in Edinburgh. He opposed the Baptists and Quakers of Terling, where he continued to minister after his ejection in 1662.

Edmund Staunton (1600-71) [Ox] WD was converted at eighteen after a serious illness and a brush with death by drowning. He studied at Gray's Inn before entering the ministry. He was very diligent in his ministry mainly at Kingston, Surrey. He gained his DD 1634. He was suspended for refusing to read the BS 1635 but in Cromwell's time he preached often before Parliament though he was against the regicide. He was appointed president of Corpus Christi, Oxford, 1648 but was ejected 1660 and silenced 1662. He continued to preach and may have had Salters' Hall, London, built for him.

Shropshire-born Rowland Stedman (d. 1673) [Ox] was a published author ejected from Wokingham, Berkshire 1662. He continued to preach after this and was one of Philip, Lord Wharton's chaplains at Wooburn, where he died 1673. L. 1672 (Presbyterian) in Buckinghamshire. His will says that in 'not conforming to ceremonies and other impositions' he was not led 'by humour, faction or any carnal interest whatsoever but as really judging such conformity sinful'.

Nathaniel Stephens (1606/7-78) [Ox, Magdalen] was a friend of Baxter's and knew George Fox the Quaker from childhood. Fox was a big influence in younger days but he later publicly opposed him as he did Baptists and others. He also published in favour of Calvinism and infant baptism and on original sin and eschatology. Ejected from Fenny Drayton, Leicestershire, 1662, he continued to preach in the Hinckley area. L. 1672 (Presbyterian) at his house.

Kendal-born John Strickland (1601?-70) [Ox, Queens] WD (from October 1643) was 'a great divine, and generally esteemed ... eminent for expounding the scriptures, and an excellent casuist' (Calamy). He served in London and elsewhere, then came to Ludlow, Shropshire, from where he was ejected 1662. He continued to preach there and elsewhere. He was father-in-law to two ejected ministers, Rosewell and William Gough (*c.* 1626 - *c.* 1692).

Gloucestershire-born Henry Stubb[e]s (1605/6-78) [Ox, Magdalen] served first in Lincolnshire then Ireland. The Irish Uprising of 1641 precipitated a move back to England. He settled in Somerset but was removed 1660. He assisted Joseph Woodward (d. 1662) at Dursley, Gloucestershire, until his ejection in 1662. In the succeeding years he preached in London and throughout the West Country. Fellow ministers commented that they had 'often known him to continue five or six hours together in preaching, chiefly in prayer on fasting-days', accomplishing this 'without impertinencies, tautologies, tedious repetitions, or any crude, raw, rude, and nauseating expressions'. L. 1672 (Presbyterian) at his own house in Jewin Street, London. On leaving London 1675, he preached a published farewell sermon: *A Dissuasive from Conformity to the World, as also God's Severity Against Impenitent*

*Sinners.* He also wrote *Conscience the Best Friend upon Earth.* Watson and Baxter preached funeral sermons for him. BF.

Maidstone-born George Swinnock (*c.* 1627-73) [Cam & Ox] ended his days in his home town. L. 1672 (Presbyterian) at High Wycombe. He is a well-known Puritan author still in print today.

Nottinghamshire-born Matthew Sylvester (1636/37-1708) [Cam] was ejected from Great Gonerby, Lincolnshire, 1662. After serving as a chaplain, he went to London 1671. L. 1672 (Presbyterian) at Coleman Street. He was on good terms with many of London's Anglican clergy, particularly Whichcote and Tillotson. He was a victim of the Hilton gang 1642 and was fined £40. Baxter worked as his assistant until his death in 1691 and then Calamy took up the position until 1695. His second wife was the daughter of ejected minister Obadiah Hughes. He published several sermons, including two volumes on *The Christian's Race* (1702-8). His chief claim to literary fame is as the editor of Baxter's autobiography, which was published 1696 as an unwieldy 900-page folio called *Reliquiae Baxterianae.* It was Calamy's efforts to rectify this mess that led to his own writings on Nonconformity.

## T

Francis Tallents (1619-1708) was based in Shrewsbury and had wide interests, including mathematics and science, and was a friend of Boyle. 'A good Scholar, a godly, blameless Divine, most eminent for extraordinary prudence and moderation, and peaceableness towards all' (Baxter). Often imprisoned after ejection in 1662, he annually observed St Bartholomew's Day as a day of humiliation and fasting.

William Thomas (1592/93-1667) was suspended for refusing to read BS 1634. When asked in 1662 his view of the Prayer Book he remarked, 'I bless God, it is so good, but yet it might be better', for which he was ejected. Ox. Oath 1666. A son was an Anglican minister.

Lancashire-born Presbyterian John Tilsley (*c.* 1614-84) was ejected 1662 but eventually conformed again 1670.

John Tombes (1602-76) [Ox, Magdalen], the accomplished linguist and celebrated Baptist was a Presbyterian until 1643 when he moved to London to consider the question of baptism. He presented an excitation and an examen on the subject to the Westminster Assembly. In 1640 he returned to Bewdley, where he served in the national church and gathered a Baptist congregation. He famously debated Baxter on baptism in 1650. From 1651 to 1660 he was based in Leominster again. Though sympathetic to the national church idea, Tombes held Baptist views that made ejection inevitable and it came in September 1662. Both conservative and radical, he regularly attended the parish church and received communion, but adhered to his tenet on infant baptism 'by going out of the church whilst that office was performing and returning in again when it was ended' (Calamy). L. 1672 at his own house in London. In his *Brief Lives* John Aubrey (1626-97) wrote of 'a little man, neat limbed, a little quick searching eye, sad, grey'.

Robert Towne (1592/93?-1664) [Ox] was an antinomian. He was imprisoned for such beliefs 1640 but continued in the Church of England until his ejection in 1662. He ministered to Dissenters until his death in Haworth, Yorkshire, two years later.

Published author William Troughton (1613/14-86/90) was ejected 1660 and became an Independent minister. He was suspected of involvement in the abortive republican Tong Plot 1662.

Joseph Truman (1631-71) [Ox], ejected 1662, was a friend of Robert Porter and wrote several books. He was a man of 'profound judgement and tenacious memory, very swift in reading books and happy in retaining what he read' who was 'often indicted' and 'once sued to an outlawry, which was very chargeable to him' but pleaded his cause so well he was acquitted (Calamy).

## U/V

Edward Veal or Veel (1632/33-1708) [Ox] became a Nonconformist tutor in Wapping after being silenced 1662. Before that he had been in Ireland as a minister and fellow of Trinity, Dublin, but had returned to London. L. 1672 (Independent). His students included Samuel Wesley (1662-1735), father of John and Charles.

Ralph Venning (c. 1622-74) [Cam, Emmanuel] was author of *Sin, the Plague of Plagues* (1691) and other books often reprinted. BF.

# W

Monmouthshire-born Henry Walter (1611-78?) [Ox] ministered there both before and after 1662 despite some strong opposition from Romanists. L. 1672 at Llantarnam.

John Warren (1621-96) was a friend of Baxter's based in Hatfield Broad Oak, Essex. He used to say that 'he would not leave Hatfield Christians for any place in England' (Calamy). He tackled Baxter on justification firmly but fairly in several personal letters

William Whitaker (d. 1672) [Cam, Emmanuel] was ejected from Bermondsey in Southwark 1662.

Henry Wilkinson was a name shared by two ejected men, neither of whom is to be confused with a Roman Catholic apologist of the same name. Henry Wilkinson (1610-75) [Ox] was a renowned preacher in Camberwell and Clapham. While a student, he was known as 'Long Harry' to distinguish him from Dean Harry, Henry Wilkinson (1616/17-90) [Ox], the then head of Magdalen, who was, after ejection, imprisoned and fined for Nonconformity.

There were also two men called Thomas Willis, one of whom was more moderate and later conformed. They are Thomas Willis (*fl.* 1618-73) and Thomas Willis (d. 1692).

## A cloud of witnesses

Such lists can make dry reading but, just as with a visit to Dunkirk, where the names recorded of those killed in battle moves us to admire their willingness to die for the cause, so, with these names, we are reminded of the faithfulness of many who, regardless of fear or favour, cast themselves on God at an important hour in the history of the nation and we are encouraged to go and do likewise.

'Such were these men,' wrote Lloyd-Jones in 1962, 'great and mighty scholars, mighty preachers, men of character and of strength of conviction, men of courage', men the memory of whom causes us to give thanks to God. 'Having seen the position clearly' they 'acted upon it at all costs. May God give us grace to follow in their train.'

(Key: [Ox] or [Cam] reveals that the man attended Oxford or Cambridge University; 'BS' = 'Book of Sports'; 'WD' = Westminster Divine, a member of the Westminster Assembly; 'Ox. Oath' means he took the Oxford Oath, the demanding oath required to escape the rigours of the Five Mile Act; 'L. 1672' means the man was licensed to preach by the indulgence of that year. 'BF' means he was buried in Bunhill Fields, London.)

# 10 | 1662 AND 2012 — SOME CONCLUDING PRACTICAL OBSERVATIONS

**W**e want in this final chapter to attempt some practical observations for today in the light of what we have learned about 1662 and what followed. I am drawing chiefly on the conclusions of Dr D. M. Lloyd-Jones in two papers he gave in 1962, the first to the Evangelical Library on 1662 itself and the second to the Puritan Conference on the period 1640-62.

In the paper on 1640-62 Lloyd-Jones points to certain mistakes on the part of the Puritans. First, the mixing of politics and faith. There are many examples of this on both sides of most questions but it is clear that attempts to rely on politics rather than on God were continually backfiring. We have said next to nothing about Puritan disunity but it is clear that this factor did not help them at all. Lloyd-Jones also raises the way that the state church idea was assumed almost without question. There are those who sincerely hold the view that the church and the state should be closely bound together, even identical or at least working in tandem. Is that really what the New Testament teaches, however? We simply raise the question.

More positively he calls upon us to learn from this history to keep preaching the gospel first and foremost, to keep such preaching central and to fight our battles in a spiritual way. With those brief lessons there are perhaps a dozen others we can list.

## Depravity and grace

It is surely not possible to read of some of the cruel acts perpetrated in this dark age that we have been looking at without being reminded once again of the depravity of man.

An outrageous act not yet touched on concerns two women — Alice Lisle and Elizabeth Gaunt. Following the inexcusable Rye House Plot, it was discovered that Alice Lisle had given refuge to some of the plotters. Badgered by Judge Jeffreys the jury reluctantly gave in a guilty verdict against her. Around the same time, Elizabeth Gaunt was also found guilty of a similar crime. Both women were burnt at the stake.

With amazing cheer and confidence, as she burned, Elizabeth Gaunt said:

> I exult that God has honoured me to be the first that is called to suffer by fire in this reign, and that my suffering is a martyrdom for that religion that is all love.

'Charity', she said,

> ... is a part of my religion, as well as faith. My crime is at worst only that of feeding an enemy, so I hope I shall have my reward

from him for whose sake I did this service, how unworthy soever the person was that made so ill a return for it.

## Conscience

The Bible speaks about the conscience often enough but it is a rather neglected subject among evangelicals today. The 1662 men were men who knew that they had a conscience and who were willing to act upon it with courage when necessary.

The story is told of how someone once said to Oliver Heywood, 'Ah, Mr Heywood, we should gladly have you preach still in our church.' He replied, 'Yes, I would as gladly preach as you can desire it, if I could do it with a safe conscience.' The man honestly replied, 'Oh, sir, many nowadays make a great gash in their consciences: cannot you make a little nick in yours?' Heywood clearly could not.

In his farewell sermon Joseph Caryl says:

> The heart or conscience is a busy faculty, and hath many offices, it records what we do, and comes as a witness. The conscience is judge of what we do, and accordingly reproves what we do amiss; therefore saith Job, 'I will take care of this:' I am more afraid of the reproach of conscience, than of any man whatsoever; therefore I will not do any thing that may cause my conscience to reproach me as long as I live. This is upon the heart of God's people, they are resolved, let men reproach and rail against them as much as they will, their hearts shall not reproach them.

Samuel Birch of Bampton in Oxfordshire wrote for himself:

> I am at thy footstool – I may not do evil that good may come – I may not do this great sin against my God and the dictates of my conscience. I therefore surrender myself, my soul, my ministry, my people, my place, my wife, and children, and whatsoever else

is here concerned, into thy hand, from whom I received them. Lord, have mercy upon me and assist me for ever to keep faith and a good conscience.

That was the attitude of the ejected men and it should be ours.

## The Reformation

Lloyd-Jones also insists that the events of 1662 force us to ask the question 'What do we think of the Protestant Reformation?' Those who were ejected were not ejected because they supported the Protestant Reformation but because they 'believed, further, that it had not gone far enough in the Church of England'.

He quotes R. S. Bosher's statement that '1662 marks the final refusal to come to terms with the Continental Reformation' and that 'Ecclesia Anglicana was of another spirit than Geneva'.

That poses a question for us: What is our view of the Reformation? Was it a mistake, as some insist? If it was right, then what about the principle it espoused, the principle not just of reformation but of going on reforming. Do we see it that way?

## Tradition

Further, what decides us as far as truth is concerned? Do we say that if we were born into a certain church, Anglican, say, or Baptist, that we simply remain with it come hell or high water? Are we free to follow a certain tradition simply because it is to us an attractive one or gives certain advantages? Or is it truth that really matters? In Lloyd-Jones' words

Am I to be influenced primarily by the fact that I happen to have been brought up in a certain denomination, or am I to be influenced primarily by the teaching of the word of God?

156

## Integrity

What about mental reservations or giving my own private interpretation to Articles or Confessions of faith that I am required to subscribe to? 'Whatever may be said against them,' says Lloyd-Jones again, 'the Puritans were honest men. They could not prevaricate, they could not indulge in mental reservations.' What about us?

## In it to win it

The Puritans tried for more than a hundred years to work within the Church of England. In 1662 the majority of them felt compelled to say enough is enough and so they were ejected. To quote Lloyd-Jones yet again:

> Their story compels all who hold their evangelical views to face this question. When do we come to the position of 1662? At what point do we feel that we are compromising the Truth and violating conscience?

The Anglican church of today is undoubtedly very different to what it was in 1662, though not all things have changed. Anyone who chooses to work within it ought to be aware of its history.

## Authority

Does the whole story not warn us to be on our guard against all authoritarian tendencies in churches, all tendencies to ecclesiasticism and hierarchical principles? Where are these found in Scripture?

## Liturgism

Should we not be very suspicious of increasing tendencies in some quarters today towards liturgism in worship and the tendency to put more emphasis on other parts of the service rather than on the sermon? Those who exalt the 'service' often do so at the expense of the sermon.

## Denials of the truth

If the 1662 men were willing to suffer in the way that they did what should be our attitude towards flagrant denials of the very foundations and first principles of the Christian faith, or the widespread indifference to doctrine which is to be found in professing churches?

The choice continues to be very much — conformity or purity?

## The example of these men

Lloyd-Jones says of the men we have been considering that

> ... above all, they have left us this noble, glorious, wonderful example of holy living, patient endurance in suffering, and loyalty to the Word of God and its message, even at the cost of being 'fools for Christ's sake' and being regarded as 'the offscourings of all things'.

A consideration of these men and the stand that they took should, at the very least, stir us to holiness, patience when we suffer and a strong commitment to being ruled by God's Word.

## Self-examination

The example of these men calls upon us to examine ourselves and to see where we stand. What is the state of the church? What about my own part in it? How can we expect God to bless us if we are not willing to ask ourselves serious questions about such things?

We trust that this book will help us all to do that.

# A TIMELINE

1593 Religion Act of Elizabeth's reign
1603 Death of Elizabeth, accession of James I
1617 'Book of Sports' first published
1620 The *Mayflower* sails to America
1625 Death of James, accession of Charles I
1639 Bishops' Wars begin
1640 *Etcetera* oath introduced
1649 Charles beheaded, beginning of the Interregnum
1643 Solemn League and Covenant, Westminster Assembly
1651 Christopher Love executed for plotting the return of the monarchy. Last of the English Civil Wars.
1653 Beginning of the Protectorate
1654 Sequestration of ministers under Cromwell
1656 The Quaker Nayler rides into Bristol
1658 Death of Oliver Cromwell, succeeded by his son Richard
1659 Richard Cromwell steps down

**1660** Charles II restored, Oblivion Act, Act for Confirming and Restoring Ministers, Worcester House Declaration, Corporation Act

**1661** Venner Uprising, Savoy Conference,

**1662** Act of Uniformity and Great Ejection, Tong Plot

**1663** Sheldon made Archbishop of Canterbury

**1664** First Conventicle Act, Charles saves Aylesbury Baptists

**1665** Five Mile Act, Great Plague, War with Dutch begins

**1666** Great Fire of London

**1670** Second Conventicle Act

**1672** Charles's Indulgence, licences sought

**1673** First Test Act

**1678** Second Test Act, 'Popish Plot'

**1680** Death of Goodwin

**1681** New wave of persecution begins

**1683** Death of Owen, James's Indulgence, Rye House Plot

**1685** Death of Charles II, accession of James II

**1688** Death of Bunyan, heir born to James

**1689** William and Mary succeed James II, Act of Toleration, Baptist Confession published

**1690** Establishment of the Common Fund to help needy Presbyterian and Independent ministers

**1691** Death of Baxter

**1692** The year of the short-lived Happy Union between Presbyterians and Independents

**1720** Death of Nathan Denton, the last of the ejected ministers to die

**1828** Repeal of Test and Corporation Acts

# APPENDIX

This list is based on Thomas Coleman and chiefly the more conservative A G Matthews. It gives the number of ministers ejected from the different counties of England, etc. The numbers in brackets refer to those who afterwards conformed and so need to be deducted.

| | |
|---|---|
| London and Westminster & Southwark | 113 (3) |
| Bedfordshire | 9 (2) |
| Berkshire | 24 (5) |
| Buckinghamshire | 30 (1) |
| Cambridgeshire | 14 |
| Channel Islands | 3 |
| Cheshire | 44 (9) |
| Cornwall | 42 (5) |
| Cumberland | 20 (2) |
| Derbyshire | 39 (4) |

| | |
|---|---:|
| Devonshire | 121 (10) |
| Dorsetshire | 52 (2) |
| Durham | 17 (6) |
| Essex | 99 (3) |
| Gloucestershire | 52 (2) |
| Hampshire | 52 (2) |
| Herefordshire | 23 (1) |
| Hertfordshire | 30 (1) |
| Huntingdonshire | 8 (2) |
| Kent | 62 (6) |
| Lancashire | 61 (5) |
| Leicestershire | 35 (3) |
| Lincolnshire | 40 (4) |
| Middlesex | 32 (2) |
| Norfolk | 60 (8) |
| Northamptonshire | 46 (7) |
| Northumberland | 34 (2) |
| Nottinghamshire | 34 (7) |
| Oxfordshire | 23 (4) |
| Rutland | 10 (3) |
| Shropshire | 36 (5) |
| Somerset | 62 (2) |
| Staffordshire | 44 (3) |
| Suffolk | 79 (12) |
| Surrey | 33 (2) |
| Sussex | 65 (1) |
| Warwickshire | 31 (2) |
| Westmorland | 14 (2) |
| Wiltshire | 60 (5) |
| Worcestershire | 35 (7) |
| Yorkshire | 110 (17) |
| **Total listed above** | **1,636 (171)** |
| North Wales | 14 |
| South Wales | 64 |
| Oxford Uni | 35 |
| Cambridge Uni | 45 |

# BIBLIOGRAPHY

## Contemporary or near contemporary items

The main items from the period worth consulting are:

1663ff, *The Farewell Sermons* (various editions especially that edited by Edmund Calamy III)

1696, Richard Baxter, *Reliquiae Baxterianae* 800-page folio autobiography, available in various, abridged editions. Part 2 deals with the period. First edition edited by Matthew Sylvester (*c.* 1636-1708)

1702-7, Edward Hyde, Duke of Clarendon, *History of the Rebellion and Civil Wars in England: Begun in the Year 1641*

1723, Gilbert Burnet, *History of his own times.* See Volume 1, Part 2. Also relevant entries in the famous Diary of Samuel Pepys 1633-1703 (and John Evelyn 1620-1706).

1862, Peter Bayne (Introduction), *Documents Relating to the Settlement* of the Church of England by the Act of Uniformity of 1662 (*English Puritanism: Its Character and History*).

## Nonconformist's Memorial

1702, Edmund Calamy III, *Abridgement of Mr Baxter's History of his Life and Times ... With an Account of the many Others ... who were Ejected after the Restauration ... And a Continuation of their History, till the Year 1691.* The account takes up the second half of the book. Calamy expanded his work in two subsequent two-volume publications.

1713, *An Abridgement ... Continuation of their History, to ... 1711*

1727, *A Continuation of the Account.*

1775, Samuel Palmer, Calamy's work was edited as *The Nonconformist's Memorial.*

1777-78, revised edition

1802, second edition in three volumes

1934, A. G. Matthews, facts verified and augmented in *Calamy Revised* (reprint 1988)

## Older Histories

1732-38, Daniel Neal, 1678-1743, *History of the Puritans*

1738, Thomas Crosby, 1685-1750, *History of the English Baptists*

1797, Joshua Toulmin, 1740-1815, revised edition of Neal in five volumes (reprinted 1822, 1844)

1812, David Bogue and James Bennett, *History of the Dissenters*

1848, John Stoughton, *Spiritual Heroes or Sketches of the Puritans*

1852, J. B. Marsden, *The History of the Later Puritans*

1862, Robert Vaughan, *History of English Nonconformity*

1862, John Waddington, *Christian Churches Congregational Church History from the Reformation to 1662*

## Other older works

1820, Benjamin Brook, *History of Religious Liberty Volume 2*

1860, Thomas Coleman, *The Two Thousand Confessors of Sixteen Hundred and Sixty-Two*

1862, Various authors, *St Bartholomew Bicentenary Papers*
1862, Various authors, *The Ejectment of 1662 and the Free Churches*
1862, Charles Stanford, *Joseph Alleine: His companions and times; A memorial of 'Black Bartholomew,' 1662*

## More recent works

1912, Benjamin A. Millard, *The Great Ejectment of 1662 and the Rise of the Free Churches*

1956, G. R. Cragg, *Puritanism in the Period of the Great Persecution 1660-1688*

1958, Robert S. Bosher, *The Making of the Restoration Settlement the Influence of the Laudians 1649-1662*

1962, E. A. Payne, N. S. Moon, *Baptists and 1662*

1962, Dr D. M. Lloyd-Jones, *1662-1962 From Puritanism to Nonconformity* (Evangelical Library Lecture); *Puritan Perplexities: Some Lessons from 1640-1662* (Puritan Conference paper)

1962, Geoffrey Nuttall and Owen Chadwick eds. *From Uniformity to Unity 1662-1962*

1968, H. G. Alexander, *Religion in England 1558-1662* (London History Studies)

1970, Paul S. Seaver, *The Puritan Lectureships: The Politics of Religious Dissent 1560-1662*

1978, Michael R. Watts, *The Dissenters 1: From the Reformation to the French Revolution*

1978, I. M. Green, *The Re-establishment of the Church of England 1660-1663*

1987, Peter Beale, *1662 and the Foundation of Non-conformity* (Westminster Conference)

1998, John Spurr, *English Puritanism 1603-1689* (Social History in Perspective Series)

2000, John Coffey, *Persecution and Toleration in Protestant England 1558-1689*

2006, David J. Appleby, *Black Bartholomew's Day Preaching, Polemic and Restoration Nonconformity*

2008, Lee Gatiss, *The Tragedy of 1662* (Latimer Paper 66)

2011, Derek Cooper, *Thomas Manton* (Guided Tour Series)